SEASON
Of Our
DREAMS

The 2010 Auburn Tigers

Books by Van Allen Plexico

The Sentinels
  When Strikes the Warlord
  A Distant Star
  Apocalypse Rising
  Alternate Visions (editor)
  The Shiva Advent
  Worldmind
  Stellarax (forthcoming)

Comics Commentary (editor)
  Assembled!
  Assembled! 2
  Assembled! 3 (forthcoming)

Lucian: Dark God's Homecoming

Hawk (forthcoming)

SEASON

Of Our

DREAMS

The 2010 Auburn Tigers

Van Allen Plexico
& John Ringer

"Wishbone" Columnists
from *TheWarEagleReader.com*

WHITE ROCKET BOOKS

Van and John would like to gratefully acknowledge and express their appreciation to Jeremy Henderson and the War Eagle Reader for publishing our original columns during the 2010 football season. Visit the site at www.thewareaglereader.com

SEASON OF OUR DREAMS: THE 2010 AUBURN TIGERS

Copyright 2011 by Van Allen Plexico and John Ringer

Photographs by Ami Plexico

Portions of this book originally appeared at the War Eagle Reader www.thewareaglereader.com

A White Rocket Book
www.whiterocketbooks.com

ISBN-13: 978-0-9841392-3-1
ISBN-10: 0-9841392-3-0

This book is set in Calibri.

First printing: February 2011

0 9 8 7 6 5 4 3 2 1

CONTENTS

To Denise, Alexandra, Gabrielle and Ethan—I never enjoyed watching a season of Auburn football more than watching this one with you.

—John

To my granddad, Joseph Lee Plexico, Sr., who didn't get to see this season, and to my dad, Joseph Lee Plexico, Jr., who did. To Ami, who jumped on board with me and shared the crazy ride; and to Maddie & Mira—here's hoping you get to see a dozen more.

—Van

Riffing on those ubiquitous Oregon play-calling cards, early in the season. It didn't take us long to figure out just what we had in 2010—and where it might lead us.

– INTRODUCTION –

This is not just a book. It's actually quite a few things, all at once.

Primarily, it is a record of the views and predictions, analysis and reactions, week by week throughout the magical 2010 season, of two Auburn alumni who also happen to be lifelong fans of the Tigers' football program.

It is also a collection of the columns those two guys wrote under the combined name of "the Wishbone" for the War Eagle Reader blog, week after week, beginning shortly after the season started.

At first, the idea was to write about a variety of topics in some way related to Auburn football. We hoped the Tigers would have a good season in 2010—hopefully one even better than the surprisingly successful 2009 campaign in new Coach Gene Chizik's first year. As the season developed, however, it became quite obvious to all concerned that this was not going to be just another "good" Auburn football season. No, 2010 rapidly shaped up to be something quite extraordinary, remarkable, and (as the weeks ticked by), increasingly spectacular.

Maybe even, the guys realized somewhere along the line as the wins kept coming and the team played better and better, *once in a lifetime* spectacular.

After all, it's not like the Tigers have, historically, put themselves in such a position every year or two.

To be an Auburn football fan is not necessarily to qualify for the infamous tag of "long-suffering;" the Tigers have won plenty of games over the years, along with seven SEC Championships and the 1957 AP National Championship, and rank somewhere between #15 and #20 in most calculations of the winningest college football programs of all time.

That being said, for over half a century after that '57 title, the Tigers seemed to be positively snake-bitten when it came to winning—or even playing for—another national championship. From being jumped by lower-ranked teams in the final polls to being on probation in undefeated years to being stuck behind two other teams all year long, anything that could go wrong usually did.

So as the 2010 season unfolded in all of its mind-blowing, eye-popping, utterly astonishing *greatness*, the two Wishbone columnists shifted their attentions more every week to the games and the players and the team itself—and to pondering the ultimate destiny that just might lie ahead for this most remarkable of all Auburn teams.

This book represents not just an after-the-fact appraisal of the 2010 season but a look into the minds and hearts of two Dye-hard Auburn men who watched it unfold before their eyes, and who wrote about each game and each week as it played out in real time, with no benefit of hindsight.

We present it to you here, warts and all, pretty much as we wrote it at the time—one column a week, one chapter at a time, all the way to the end.

We hope it brings back some warm memories and may eventually serve as one more souvenir of a year that took us all by surprise, turned our world upside down, and gave us a season of our dreams.

--Van Allen Plexico & John Ringer—
"The Wishbone"
January 2011

– PRE-SEASON AND ARKANSAS STATE WEEK –

We Didn't Know What We Were In For!

For Auburn Tigers fans worldwide, 2010 represented nothing less than the season of our dreams.

After so many years of near-misses and disappointments and circumstances beyond our control, the stars finally aligned for Auburn and the Tigers took home the ultimate prize in college football.

Honestly, this season seemed to come out of nowhere. No reasonable observer really expected Auburn to make it through the regular season undefeated (though several of Phil Steele's models did predict that the Tigers would be undefeated going to Tuscaloosa in the final week of the season). Few thought Auburn would have any chance of winning when they traveled to Tuscaloosa for the final game of the regular season. Nobody expected that Auburn would not only win the SEC West and make it to Atlanta for the SEC Championship Game, but that the Tigers would also blow out a Steve Spurrier-coached team when they got there—breaking scoring records in the process.

Even more improbably, nobody expected that the Tigers should have a season like this the very next season after Alabama had accomplished the very same things. Tide fans, who notoriously place so much of their personal self-worth and self-esteem in the

11

basket of University of Alabama football success, had mere months earlier been crowing to the heavens that the Tide's success in claiming the Heisman Trophy (their first) for running back Mark Ingram and a BCS title in Pasadena indicated that nature and nature's God intended for the Crimson Tide to always stand triumphant over Auburn—indeed, over all of the college football landscape. Some Tide fans went so far as to assert that Auburn was "not a big-time program like Alabama" and would "never win a national championship," despite Auburn's overall better record nationally, in the conference, and head-to-head with Alabama over the three decades since the Bear's demise.

Thus 2010 couldn't have been more shocking and surprising to them if the Rapture itself had occurred, complete with the good lord coming down to announce that Auburn fans were somehow the equal of their crimson-clad counterparts in the state.

In retrospect, however, Auburn's year of dominance might have been foreseen if one considered how Auburn so often seems to replicate the exceptional accomplishments—for good or ill—happening on the other side of the state. A couple of examples:

In 1992, Alabama culminated a three-year rise under Gene Stallings with a 13-0 season and SEC and national titles. Meanwhile, Auburn had just closed out Pat Dye's career with a last-two-years mark of ten wins, eleven losses, and a draw. Auburn's hiring of new head coach Terry Bowden from Samford scarcely struck fear into the hearts of Tide supporters. On top of everything else, the Tigers were placed on two years of probation prior to the start of the 1993 season, including post-season and television bans.

Of course the Tigers responded with an undefeated 11-0 season, right on the heels of Alabama's own, and a win in the Iron Bowl over the defending champs.

At the other end of the spectrum, something similar happened in 1997-98. Alabama's team collapsed in 1997 and finished with a record of 4-7, while Auburn was winning the West and playing in its first SEC title game ever. And yet, the very next year, it was Auburn collapsing and ending the year with only three wins. Truly, geographic proximity is only the beginning when it comes to the strange and sometimes utterly bizarre connection between the two programs.

That brings us back to 2010. During the long offseason, Alabama was riding high, still basking in the glow of their BCS National Championship, their trophy on display at Wal-Marts across Alabama. The multitudes of crimson-clad fans who had possessed so little worth cheering about for so long, prior to the hiring of Nick Saban, at last could release their long-pent-up frustrations and once again lord it over their "little brothers" to the east. Saban the savior had ended the unthinkable, six-game losing streak to the Tigers in grand style the previous year, had run off the Auburn coach (Tuberville) who had been the mastermind of that streak, and now he had taken them to the summit of the only sport that matters in the state of Alabama. Auburn, seemingly in a panic, had reached out and hired a coach from Iowa State who had a career mark as a head coach of 5-19.

The Tide fans loved it, they lived for it, and they fully intended and expected that this dominance—nationally, and over their rivals on the Plains—should last for many years to come.

Little did they dream—little did almost *anyone* dream—of what lay in store, only a few short months in the future.

Somehow nearly everyone (except your intrepid Wishbone columnists!) had forgotten that Gene Chizik had been defensive coordinator of a 13-0 Auburn squad in 2004, and then gone to Texas to pull off the exact same feat the following season—complete with a BCS National Championship victory over USC. Focusing on the 5-19 mark at Iowa State was like focusing on the first year of Saban's tenure at Alabama and declaring him a bust. It was ludicrous.

Chizik brought in a remarkable collection of assistant coaches, notably including offensive mastermind Gus Malzahn and charismatic recruiters Trooper Taylor and Curtis Luper, and together they hit the recruiting trail in a big way (indeed, eventually the NCAA would disallow some of their more visible antics, such as the famous/infamous "Tiger Prowl" in limos and Hum-Vees). Very quickly, Auburn's recruiting rankings were drawing even with—or even surpassing—Alabama's own.

And one recruit in particular would ultimately make the difference in carrying Auburn to the very brink of immortality in 2010: a junior college quarterback who had played sparingly his freshman year at Florida. When Cameron Newton signed with Auburn at the end of 2009, Tigers fans were excited at the possibilities this big, powerful, and mobile quarterback offered at the helm of Malzahn's offense. If Malzahn could make Chris Todd look so good in 2009, the Tiger faithful asked one another, just what could he do with this raw but insanely talented young man?

What he did with him exceeded everyone's expectations—and did so by leaps and bounds.

We don't need to go into that here. We all know. It's very likely why you're reading this book to begin with.

At the time, however, no one really knew what Cam Newton was capable of. We watched him in the A-Day spring game and almost universally proclaimed him the weakest of the four quarterbacks, in terms of passing ability. We worried that he would be designated the starter based purely on *potential*, only to falter in actual competition, leading to a quarterback controversy as the coaches frantically sent in Barrett Trotter or Clint Moseley. We fretted that perhaps the Tigers would be better off starting a more accurate passer from the beginning, rather than a more mobile running threat, despite the fact that bruising running back Ben Tate had graduated and left the Auburn running game with a limited set of options to turn to: only the fumble-prone Mario Fannin, tiny scat-back Onterrio McCalebb, and true freshman Mike Dyer.

Alabama fans chimed in at this point: Newton will be a bust, they promised. He's never seen an SEC defense. (Somehow they forgot he'd played sporadically at Florida his freshman year, and thus had indeed seen SEC defenses.)

One can scarcely blame them, though. No one had quite imagined what was to come—on the ground or by the air—from the big man with the big smile and the "2" on his jersey.

So when the Arkansas State game at last rolled around, kicking off the 2010 season, Auburn fans looked on with perhaps greater than usual interest, anxious to see what Newton could do—but just as interested in seeing five-star recruit Mike Dyer in action, not to mention the other highly-touted rookies joining the team. The season was viewed initially as another building year, with the opportunity for true greatness still at least a couple of years away. The team's slogan was "Good to Great"—but that was generally interpreted by many as a goal to strive for, if unlikely to actually reach. Many hoped the 2010 Tigers would increase their win total from the previous year's eight to perhaps nine or ten, though hardly anyone thought they could do much better than that. Certainly with mighty Alabama holding sway over their division, along with an always-powerful LSU, rapidly improving Arkansas, and newly invigorated Mississippi State, the mountain any other challenger would have to climb was incredibly immense.

The Arkansas State game both encouraged and discouraged Tigers fans. The offense looked good—and Cam Newton exploded for his first long touchdown run in this game. The defense, however, allowed Arkansas State to pass up and down the field, surrendering 26 points. Fans fretted and experts pontificated: No team with such a porous secondary could realistically challenge in any conference or division—particularly not in what was clearly the best division of the best conference in all of college football.

And just ahead lay a conference game against a rapidly-improving team in their home stadium, with a very tough defense and a coach considered among the brightest young minds in the game.

What was this Auburn team made of? We would begin to find that out in a hurry—starting on a Thursday night in Starkville, Miss.

So the opening game was in the books, and Auburn fans were in a stir. Half the talk was about the enormous potential we were just beginning to glimpse from one Cameron Newton. The other half of the talk consisted of serious misgivings about the state of our pass defense. The typical comment went something like, "If Arkansas State can do that to our defense, what will_____ do to us?"

Indeed, the defensive secondary would remain a concern for most of the rest of the season. Even in games that Auburn won, the opponent was never shut down and shut out by that Big Blue Defense the way we had become accustomed to in our previous memorable seasons. No, this Auburn team would have to outscore its foes to win—and, as it turned out, we had the offense to do just that.

There's an old maxim of football: "Defense wins championships." But 2010 would prove that even the oldest of truisms have their exceptions. While ultimately the Auburn defense would acquit itself as a powerful and fearful unit, particularly up front (and as personified by eventual Lombardi Award winner Nick Fairley), there would be no doubt about what the dominant aspect of the 2010 Tigers would be: that amazing offense, which had only begun to reveal its awesome might that first week.

The Mississippi State game gave us all pause. The Bulldogs held Auburn to only seventeen points. We worried that perhaps this year's team represented something of a regression from 2009—we had lost the powerful Ben Tate, after all.

How little we knew then...!

Meanwhile, somewhere around this time, a photo surfaced of a football helmet with the traditional "AU" logo on the side... but the helmet itself was blue. Blue. And just like that, all conversation turned to the old debate between Auburn uniform "purists" and those wanting more variety in the Tigers' look. The Wishbone, naturally enough, joined in with a little look at history...

Uniform Opinion?

Sudden and dramatic changes to a football team's uniform: A bold and ingenious motivational move by forward-thinking and clever coaches, or a cynical and outright obnoxious ploy that verges on desperation, and actually does more harm than good to a program?

There's no doubt which side of that question most Auburn fans come down on. Few college football programs have stuck with their basic uniform/helmet look more persistently over the decades than has Auburn. Yet despite that overwhelming preference among the Auburn Family, there have been changes—some temporary, some permanent—here and there.

As rumors once again swirl that this weekend could see a surprise change (Blue pants? Blue helmets? What—are we the UN Peacekeeping Force suddenly?), it's worth a quick look back at the changes that worked—and the ones that didn't.

Somewhere in the 1960s, or so the story goes, Shug Jordan got together with Athletics Director Jeff Beard to come up with a logo for the helmets. Jordan actually wanted to put an eagle on there, but Beard rejected that notion.

Van says: You think other schools' fans get confused by our "Tiger/Eagle" business now? Imagine if we were continuing to insist

17

that we are the Tigers-- but we had a freakin' eagle on our helmets! Yeah, that would have cleared things right up.

Beard, bless his heart, instead experimented with stencils and came up with the interlocking AU logo that we all know and love today. Yes, the ubiquitous AU logo actually began on the helmets before spreading everywhere else.

Van says: Except for the band's uniforms, as my wife pointed out last week, and for which I had no real answer. Where did their eagle-head "A" come from, and why is it so different? Perhaps it pre-dates the interlocking AU?

John says: Here is all you need to know about the importance of the AU logo. When they made the sticker on the helmets slightly larger for this year's A-Day game, we had a big debate in my house about whether that was a good idea.

Van says: One more thing. When I briefly worked at AU Printing Services in the early Nineties, the administration considered changing the AU logo to a different design—one that would say "Auburn" to a national audience more loudly and clearly than the one we'd already been using for decades. Yeah, genius move. They actually sent out a big color sheet of alternate choices (all hideous) for employees to vote on. I returned my ballot with no choice marked, but with a write-in note: "Change the AU logo and I will consider setting fire to Samford Hall." I still wonder what would have happened to me if Samford Hall had actually caught fire that week.

The next change of note came in the late 1970s when Doug Barfield rolled out the infamous orange jerseys on four occasions. The first use of the "Barfields," against a powerhouse Georgia team in 1978, saw Auburn pull off a shocking draw. Clearly this inspired Coach B to bust them out three more times before his tenure ended at the close of the 1980 season, but never to such a positive result again. No wonder the orange "Barfields" carry such negative baggage in the minds of many Auburn fans: as with the gas lines of the Jimmy Carter years, they have become emblematic of dark days best left forgotten.

John says: In terms of pure football strategy, we have to ask: Does the "different-colored jersey" tactic result in an unexpected win more than thirty percent of the time? I have searched for statistical trends nationwide and have not found them but Auburn certainly didn't benefit, and Notre Dame doesn't do well most of the time when they go to their celebrated green jerseys. And we all remember what bama did to Georgia when the Dawgs pulled one of their "blackouts" against the Tide last year. It mostly resulted in the Dawgs blacking out.

Van says: I can see doing things before and during a game that are not directly related to wins and losses, such as changing the pre-game music or doing flyovers or whatnot. But the team's uniform is so intrinsically related to the team itself, and thus to winning and losing... it's hard to argue that changing it has any other purpose than to try to affect the outcome.

Upon taking the helm prior to the 1981 season, Pat Dye vowed to stick with the traditional look. He actually did, however, make two somewhat minor changes. First, following the Sugar Bowl win in January of 1984, he changed the facemasks from orange to dark blue. No one much complained.

John says: Many people love the orange facemasks and want to see them come back for a game. I vote no.

Van says: How the players managed to see where they were going with those bright orange grids glowing before their eyes like Three Mile Island melting down was always a mystery to me.

Throughout the 1980s, Dye only put players' names on the backs of their jerseys for bowl game trips. In all games prior to the bowls, the jerseys bore only their numbers. This changed in the early 1990s—1991, possibly—and most likely due to pressure during recruiting, when AU players suddenly got to sport their names on their backs for every game. That same effect—a deal-breaker demand voiced by many highly-ranked recruits—is the reason given by Coach Chizik for allowing multiple players to be assigned the same number on his two Auburn squads to date.

Van says: Interestingly enough, both of Dye's changes have remained in place to this day. Such was Dye's power and influence at the end of the Eighties, he probably could have rolled out pink fluffy slippers for the players and fans would have embraced them.

Terry Bowden claimed to understand the power of Auburn traditions and for the most part he didn't tamper with them, aside from changing the font used to spell out "Auburn" and "Tigers" in the end zones; he went with a fancier, baseball-jersey-looking font that provoked the ire of many fans.

Van says: It speaks volumes with regard to his standing among much of the fan base that he could get on their bad side so dramatically just by changing an end zone font.

John says: How dare he change the end zone font?!

The one somewhat major uniform change he made was to add an orange drop-shadow beneath the numbers on the jerseys during the 1996 season. Fans, however, largely rejected the look and it was gone the next year (and then so was Bowden, a year later).

Van says: I actually loved the orange drop-shadow. Call me a heretic.

John says: You're a heretic.

There haven't been any major or even minor uniform changes in the years since. Rumors swirled at the start of the 2000 season that Tommy Tuberville had orange jerseys hanging in the locker room to bust out at the start of the Wyoming game, but when the team emerged from the tunnel, they were clad in the traditional blue as always. The story goes that someone "higher up in the chain of command" nixed the idea. These "Barfield's Revenge" rumors surfaced again from time to time but Tuberville, for whatever reason, always resisted the impulse—or was told to.

And now we see the rumor mill chugging along once again, fueled in large part by the die-hard conservative, traditional nature of so many Auburn fans and alumni.   This time we're hearing about alleged blue pants, for one thing.   Blue pants with blue jerseys? Honestly, same-color jerseys and pants smacks of "Conference USA" foolishness to many.   That look carries with it the (thin) air of the WAC. It evokes images of Johnny-come-lately teams that only recently emerged into the upper echelons of football after laboring for decades in what we used to call 1-AA, and clearly missed the memo that big-boy football does not countenance the "pajamas" look.

Van says: For the most egregious example of just how catastrophically wrong it can be for an SEC team to wear this look, see the mid-Eighties Tennessee teams that dared to combine light-orange pants with their light-orange jerseys and white helmets. Good lord! It looked like they went swimming up to their necks in Velveeta.

Finally, we're now seeing a mysterious image of a fancy blue Auburn helmet, which appeared days ago on the Net as if it had fallen pristine out of the sky, or had been dropped off by a flying saucer on the way to Neptune. Wither this blue helmet? Fans are beside themselves; they search for signs and portents; they scry sheep intestines and turtle shells and the I Ching for answers to this cosmic mystery.

John: If the "blue helmet photo" (which will soon be enshrined alongside the Zapruder film) is not real then someone went to a lot of effort to create a good hoax. The helmet has the proper stickers in place and the photo was taken on carpet that looks like the Auburn equipment room. And Chizik is toying with the media and the fans about it – something I never thought he would do about anything.

Van: I don't know what to think. Is it a prototype? If so, that means someone somewhere in a position of authority has at least somewhat considered the idea of blue helmets. Do I like them? I'm not sure. Adding them to the existing home outfit doesn't work for me. I think they'd look best on the road, over a white jersey and blue pants. And, having said that, now John probably won't speak to me for a month. Ah, well.

Will we see a blue-hatted team facing orange-domed Clemson on Saturday? The Chiz swears not. But then, what's with the blue helmet? What future development does it perhaps herald? And, perhaps most significantly, will it be seen as emblematic of Chizik's power and popularity that he can foist it upon us and make us like it—or will it be held up in decades to come as an indicator of the beginning of the end; as Chizik's orange "Barfields?" Only time—and results on the field, of course—will tell.

And so Auburn had gone on the road and faced a conference and division opponent—one that had been looking toward the Auburn game as its chance to make a big splash on ESPN on a Thursday night—and had escaped with a win. A narrow one, yes, but a win all the same.

Perhaps the biggest story to emerge from this game was the advent of one Nick Fairley as a force to be reckoned with on the defensive line. After having done very little of note in 2009, Fairley exploded against the Bulldogs in Starkville, recording numerous sacks and tackles for loss, along with (of all things) an interception. Auburn was now blessed with a phenomenal playmaker on both sides of the ball, and the future Lombardi Award winner would make life exceptionally difficult for opposing quarterbacks in the weeks to come.

That game having been a Thursday night affair, we all had a couple of extra days to think about the upcoming clash with Clemson—a team Auburn had faced and defeated fairly recently, in the Chik-Fil-A Bowl following the 2007 season. (The Tigers had also defeated Clemson in the same bowl in the same venue following the 1997 season, in Dameyune Craig's final game.)

A lot of the talk in the days leading up to the Clemson game focused not on the contest itself but on the impending visit of ESPN GameDay to the Loveliest Village. It had been a while since Chris Fowler and Kirk Herbstreit and Lee Corso and the rest had come to the Plains to do their show. The overall impression was that Auburn was on the right track—reestablishing the program among the nation's best—and that ESPN was acknowledging that fact.

We didn't yet realize just how special this team was, and how special this season would be, so—as strange as it might seem in *retrospect—it was still possible at that point in the year to be distracted by such peripheral matters.*

Thinking about GameDay's previous visits, Van was reminded of an incident just before the 1995 Iron Bowl –the incident that soured his view of otherwise likeable host Chris Fowler. Van mentioned the incident to the editor of the War Eagle Reader *and was asked to write it up as a column—thus beginning this whole crazy "Wishbone" business. Here's that incident as Van remembers it nowadays.*

The GameDay Experience: Iron Bowl 1995

The impending arrival of the ESPN College GameDay crew for Saturday's clash with Clemson has me waxin' all nostalgic, back to the first time I can recall showing up to see Fowler and Corso and company live and in person: the 1995 Iron Bowl at Jordan-Hare Stadium.

I was by that point well into year nine of my Eight Year Plan for earning college degrees and obtaining student tickets—with the emphasis probably more on the student tickets, to be honest. So I had no business trying to squeeze in with a bunch of undergrads nearly ten years younger than me, just for the sake of yelling and booing on cue for the ESPN cameras. No business at all.

Nevertheless, my roommate and I decided to go. After all, if you're going to stretch the College Experience out as unnaturally long as I was already doing, what was one more largely inappropriate activity? And who could pass up the chance to boo Corso in person? (We were still a year away from the addition of Herbstreit to the crew.)

Things got stranger before Saturday had even arrived, when I found out that I had won a contest sponsored by Stouffer's frozen dinners. Part of the prize was breakfast at the Stouffer's corporate tent prior to the game. Who knew there was a Stouffer's tent outside Jordan-Hare? Not me. But as my roommate and I made our

25

way through the ocean of RVs and early-game-morning bleary-eyed crowds, heading for the GameDay set, we detoured over to said tent and, clad in our wrinkled t-shirts and jeans, joined the suit-and-tie-clad Stouffer execs (who never fully grasped exactly who we were supposed to be, nor exactly why we were crashing their corporate event) for a lovely pre-game meal of (I kid you not) Stouffer's frozen dinner food. You'd think they'd at least let the big shots eat real food at an outing like that.

There were only so many odd and uncomfortable glances we could tolerate while chewing on rubbery chicken and rice. And since time was mercifully drawing near for the GameDay telecast to begin, we bid adieu to our clueless corporate hosts and hurried through the rapidly-swelling orange-and-blue multitudes, pausing only to hurl insults at the occasional crimson-clad interloper. My secret weapon was rolled up and stashed in my pants—a sign I had cleverly fashioned to include the requisite letters "ESPN" while also being football- and GameDay-relevant, *and* insulting Lee Corso.

We wormed our way through the throngs of our fellow fans, the wind picking up and carrying a slight chill—though nothing to match the insanely intense, freezing cold of the Georgia game a week earlier, at which I had seriously contemplated lighting a section of the fabled Sanford Hedges on fire to warm myself. Somehow we managed to position ourselves just behind the GameDay set—it was, if I recall correctly, on the lawn near the Nicholls Center, where the West Stands entrance was grandly visible in the distance. From our location we couldn't see a thing the hosts were doing; other than having a small TV monitor set up nearby, to give us the frontal view from the cameras, all we could see were the backs of their chairs and heads. But that didn't matter, because we were only a scant few feet away from them, and we would be on TV! Okay, *maybe* we would be on TV. It depended on the angle the cameras shot at, and as I discovered much later, watching on tape, we were not at all on TV. But it was worth a try; and when you're a college student—even a 27 year old one!—such things somehow seem to matter a great deal.

We stood there, elbow to elbow and shoulder to shoulder with fellow fanatics, in that weird state where part of your body is sweating and the rest is freezing. Through several segments we waited, never quite sure what was going on but just living in the moment of *This is GameDay and We Are On It!,* and then they went to a commercial and some of the guys around us started yelling unintelligibly at Fowler and Corso. I couldn't tell exactly what they were saying, but then Fowler turned around and suddenly he was looking directly at me and my roommate. He gave us the most condescending smile imaginable and said in a voice just loud enough for the folks right around us to hear: "You don't really want to know what I think of this place."

Oh. My. Goodness. He. Did. Not. Just. Say. That.

My roomie and I gawked at each other while grumbles erupted in the immediate vicinity. Oh, for a "hot mike" moment. Alas, aside from the couple dozen of us located just behind him, no one else had heard it.

When the cameras came back up, I was fuming and decided it was time to unveil my sign. At that point, though, I was wishing I could somehow refashion it to make fun of Fowler. Nonetheless, I held it up, right behind Fowler's head.

Immediately, a security guard shoved his way over to me and snatched it away. I was shocked! Had the guy even had time to read it? Was he going to stuff it in the trash? Did he know that I'd spent...well, whole *minutes* thinking up its message, and then scrawling it down in magic marker on taped-together printer paper?

This was simply too much to bear. First, to hear our town and university and people dissed en masse by Fowler—a guy I'd really liked and respected up till then—and now to have my sign confiscated by the cops!

I moped. Dejected, I started to grab my roomie by the arm and gesture for us to head for the stadium.

But wait! Someone to my right was nudging me and pointing. "Hey, buddy," he said, "Corso has your sign!"

I looked over at the small TV monitor that was set up nearby and, sure enough, Corso was holding up my taped-together sign and grinning. There, displayed for everyone to see on national television—held aloft by the person it maligned, no less!—were the bright red words, "LEE CORSO PICKS HIS NOSE."

"My favorite sign of the year," Corso proclaimed to loud whoops and cheers from the crowd.

Vindication!

27

So, if you are a proud Auburn man or woman, before you go hating on Corso for all of his admittedly egregious anti-Auburn moments over the years, and before you go praising Chris Fowler for his silky-smooth studio presence, just bear in mind the events of that breezy November day on the Plains in 1995. Chris Fowler couldn't resist taking a cheap shot at his hosts, while Lee Corso had the class to laugh not at us but at himself, and to be cool about it.

Fifteen years later, that memory still stands out for me well beyond anything from the game.

Okay, well, except maybe for big Freddie "my favorite rooms are" Kitchens, impotently hurling the ball through the back of the end zone to finalize our 31-27 victory. I mean, come on—it was the Iron Bowl, after all.

In retrospect, the Clemson game was much closer than it should have been. Auburn hadn't begun to find its true strength and power on offense, and the defense was still struggling mightily with teams who could execute an effective short-passing game and could utilize small but quick players on offense to maximum effect. Meanwhile, Clemson was probably never as good again the rest of the season, particularly on offense, as they were the night of the Auburn game.

The result was a contest filled with drama, and an amazing comeback by the Tigers that would end up serving as a template for several more remarkably improbable come-from-behind wins.

And Van didn't see it until a few hours after it was over.

Every season, Van accompanies his wife to at least one game at the stadium of her alma mater, Southern Illinois, in Carbondale, Illinois. In 2010, they decided to go on the same day as the Auburn-Clemson contest. In fact, the games were played at almost the same time, meaning that Van was reduced to trying to hear the game broadcast on his iPhone (which never did work; apparently all the Auburn Network stations were blacking out the game over the Internet) or at least following the score via an ESPN app. Thus Van found himself spending much of the Southern Illinois game staring down at his phone. As both games wore on, both Auburn and SIU fell behind to their opponents; the difference was that only Auburn was able to come back.

With SIU having lost their game, Van and his wife were filing out of the stadium surrounded by other sad Saluki fans, all lamenting the tragedy of the outcome and staring glumly down at the ground. Then suddenly Van saw the Auburn score line go up... and up... and up... and he let out a cry of happiness and waved his arms in celebration—only to be met by the shocked and uncomprehending stares of the surrounding crowd of SIU fans. All seemed to be *thinking at him, all at once, "Just what are you so happy about, buddy?"*

The one-and-a-half hour drive home from Carbondale saw Van desperately trying to monitor the reports from overtime on his phone, while simultaneously trying not to drive his car off the road. At one point he actually had to pull the car over in the middle of nowhere, just to sort through Clemson's field goal / penalty / missed field goal. He wasn't entirely convinced Auburn had actually won until he got home and finished watching the recording of the game at about 2 a.m. And even then, it still seemed so improbable.

Little did he know what the rest of the season would hold...!

– SOUTH CAROLINA WEEK –

Things We Think We Know

Two big (but not huge) games in two weeks. Two three-point wins. Consternation and jubilation equally rampant among most members of the Auburn Family. Lots of, "Yes, we won, buuuut..." Nine more games directly ahead of us, six of which will determine how this season will be remembered.

We look at the results so far and we find ourselves filled with questions: Why is the offense so inconsistent? Can the defense hold up? How good was Mississippi State? How good was Clemson? And, most importantly—just how good is Auburn, really?

Lots of questions, yeah. But—what about answers? What, in fact, do we *know* so far? Or, at least, what do we *think* we know?

Here are Five Things the Wishbone *Thinks* We Know So Far:

1. The Auburn offense is both better and worse than last year. But hey, the defense is way better—right?

To quote a certain Mr. Not-Wearing-Aubie's-Head-*Ever*: "Not so fast, my friend."

When you actually compare Auburn's stats through the first three games of 2009 with the first three games of this season, some interesting and rather odd factoids become apparent. One: We are averaging ten points less per game this year (32 vs. 42 last year). Two: Rushing yards are almost the same, but passing yards are down by fifty yards (201 vs. 251 last year). Three: We're averaging 64 plays a game, vs. 81 at this point last year. (How much did the infamous "slowing it down" in Starkville contribute to that?) And four: Our turnover margin was +7 last year at this point; this year it's -4. That's an eleven-turnover swing through just three games!

So, yeah—the offense isn't quite where it was at this time a year ago. Interestingly enough, they're gaining slightly fewer total yards but more yards per play. Of course, variables have to be included such as who we played, where we played them, and so on. But the matchups are actually remarkably similar. Both years Auburn started with a non-conference patsy, followed by Miss. State, and then an out-of-conference BCS –quality foe. (Say what you will, but West Virginia was actually ranked when we played them; Clemson was not.)

The defense, on the other hand, is where we expected to find a real discrepancy. Surely, we thought as we looked at the numbers, this year's defense is easily besting the numbers of last year's much-maligned squad.

Well, guess what. The numbers given up by the 2009 and 2001 Auburn Tigers on defense are virtually *identical,* right down to the same number of sacks (seven) and the same yards per play allowed (just under five). Last year through this point we had allowed a few more rushing yards, while this year we've allowed a few more passing yards. The end result is an improvement of only *ten yards* in total defense. Oh, and we're one point better, on average, this year. This is the marked improvement many of us have been thinking we've been seeing? Really?

One conclusion that can be drawn from this is that what we really need is a good drenching downpour before and during the South Carolina game, a la West Virginia last year, hopefully leading to lots of Garcia interceptions and Lattimore fumbles and getting us back into the black in our turnover margin. That number is probably the single most glaringly negative statistic of all, and Chizik must know it, because he's started talking "increased turnover creation" with reporters. That's a good thing.

2. Clemson may finish the year with a better overall record than Auburn, and might well win the ACC.

Because they play in a weaker conference to begin with, and because the ACC this year in particular is suffering through a horrific collapse, Clemson looks as likely as anyone to take the title. They showed us something Saturday night. They came into Jordan-Hare and stood toe to toe with Auburn and rolled out SEC-caliber offensive and defensive lines, an excellent (and tough) quarterback, two good running backs and one great safety. And they were well coached. That is more than enough to win the ACC. They simply look like a rougher, tougher team—more "Man enough," as Coach Dye would put it—than they used to. They increasingly look like a real football team—an SEC team—living in a basketball conference. We will be interested to see how Clemson does when they play Miami at home in two weeks. (Heck, when the topic is "Miami gets it handed to them," we're always interested. We still remember 1983.)

3. Dr. Gustav may be outsmarting himself.

Auburn's Offensive Coordinator, Gus Malzahn, scripts the first fifteen to twenty plays of each game. It makes sense to do this because it allows him to pick good plays to start the game but more importantly to see how the other team lines up when he shows those formations , so that can line up that way again and then attack the weakness the other team is showing. There's just one problem with this: If the other team is very well-prepared for what you do, then every play and formation is perfectly defended—and that is what Clemson did early in the game. Auburn did not come off the script and start throwing downfield, and the result was a quarter and a half with no first downs. The Tigers are going to need to be more unpredictable on offense this week against a well-coached South Carolina defense.

4. The "Power Rankings" for this point in the season are pretty clear and obvious. Right?

Here is our quick-and-dirty look at who's better than whom, right now. This is not "who will win the SEC" but simply "who's better than whom."

The Elite: Alabama. And lord, how it continuously hurts to have to admit that. But it's so glaringly obvious. So we cling to hope. We try to work out elaborate scenarios whereby an Arkansas team with no running game can rack up points on the Tide, and how an Arkansas team with a weak-but-improving defense can somehow hold the Evil Elephantine Juggernaut to only a paltry few points. Oh, come on. We all know the truth—the Tide is going to crush Arkansas again. But we cling to the hope, to the false illusion, because it makes us happier. Ugh.

The Very Good: Arkansas, South Carolina, Florida, Auburn. And let's just say the two halves of The Wishbone don't exactly see eye to eye on that. One of us would drop the pulled pork below the McNuggets and drop Auburn down to the next level altogether. Speaking of which:

The Might Be Good: LSU, Kentucky, Georgia. What do we really know about LSU yet? Or about Kentucky? We ought to know plenty about Georgia by now—they've played (and lost) two league games already. And yet...there's a nagging suspicion that they could end the year with a somewhat decent record. Judging by this ranking, they've lost to the second and third best teams in the entire conference. Not a lot of shame in that—unless you're a Dawg who was entertaining lofty and clearly unrealistic dreams and expectations of titles in 2010. In which case, ouch.

The Not Good: MSU, Tennessee, Vanderbilt. Ahh, Other Bulldogs... your destiny appeared to hold such grand promise a mere two weeks ago, when the future was rosy and the loss column was empty. Whither your dreams of relevance now? Cowbells are not the magical cure for everything you hoped they would be, and after five interceptions in Red Stick, reality has re-imposed itself with a vengeance. And yet, for all that, somehow, things could be worse. Which brings us to:

The Wretched: Ole Miss. About which, the less said, the better.

5. We still have a lot of bullets in our gun that we haven't fired yet.

While the Auburn offense might currently be a riddle wrapped in a mystery encased in an enigma, one fact we can doggedly cling to is that there are still a lot of potential weapons that have scarcely seen the field. Where to begin? Alleged phenom-waiting-to-happen Trovon Reed stuck a couple of toes in the water against Clemson but claims his knee is at best 80 percent healthy. We anxiously await the earth-shattering impact (boom!) of Big Ladarious Phillips at fullback. Our tight end is a no-show, at least as far as pass-catching goes. For whatever reasons, Mario Fannin hasn't worked out as the go-to tailback, and his injury while playing that role has now unfortunately removed him from his far more effective spot as a pass-catcher out of the backfield or H-spot. With the exception of a couple of big plays, the majority of the receiving corps seems to be in the role of "provide a diversion to help Darvin Adams get open." And we're only now beginning to see some of Mike Dyer's potential.

So, yeah—lots of bullets left unfired so far. If Auburn's offense is like Christmas morning, so far we've only unwrapped a couple of packages. And that is a very encouraging thought, indeed.

So there we go—five things we think we know, or maybe five things we know we think, about the 2010 Auburn Tigers thus far. Obviously, there are still far more questions than answers hovering around this team. But there's also a lot of football left to be played, a lot more answers waiting to be discovered, and a lot more presents waiting to be opened.And by the way—we originally intended to list ten things we thought we knew... but we discovered halfway through that we only knew half as much as we thought we did.

The South Carolina game was, according to various quotes and reports, the week when the Auburn players and coaches themselves began to really believe that this could be a special team and a very special season.

This was the game in which Cam took off on that amazing run down the right sideline, culminating with a Superman-meets-Michael Jordan leap from the vicinity of the seven yard line into the end zone. Photoshopped pictures appeared immediately with Cam now sporting a red cape as he flew over the goal line.

This was also the week that the Wishbone columnists began to believe. Van had said all along that wins over both Clemson and South Carolina were unlikely; that the Tigers would surely drop one of the two. With the win over Clemson the previous week (and particularly with it coming in such onerous fashion), a Gamecock victory appeared a sure thing.

Yet somehow the Tigers won both, and pushed on into Louisiana-Monroe week still undefeated. The tiny embers of hope that every college football fan carries deep inside began to spring into actual flames. If we could beat South Carolina—and hold the mighty Marcus Lattimore to a scant few yards in the process—what else might the Tigers be capable of in 2010?

The future suddenly appeared very bright indeed...

– LOUISIANA-MONROE WEEK –

Winner Winner Chicken Dinner

Some quick hits and bullet points culled from during and after Auburn's win over the Gamecocks:

* Looking at Auburn's win over South Carolina through the side-mirror on the Wishbone's car: It was big, yeah—but, later in the year, **it will probably be even bigger than it now appears**. Why? Several reasons come to mind.

1) Given Florida's semi-struggles, South Carolina was arguably playing the best football of any team in the SEC East. And the Tigers ran wild on them. Literally *ran* wild, ringing them up for thirty-five points, mostly on the ground. Georgia, by way of contrast, could only manage six against the Gamecocks. *Six.*

2) When the time comes to divvy up the bowl games, and modestly assuming Auburn finishes with a good but not spectacular record (though, hey, you can't blame hopes for soaring a bit this week!), winning this game could make the difference between a December bowl and New Year's Day again. We can hardly count on a repeat of last year's bizarre statistical anomaly where nearly every team in the SEC not named "Alabama" finished with virtually

identical records, sending us to Tampa at 7-5. So this win could be a real difference-maker in that regard.

3) While Auburn is now 6-10 all-time against Steve Spurrier-coached teams, the Tigers have not lost to the Ol' Ball Coach in this century. (2000 was technically the last year of the Twentieth Century.) The bulk of the losses-- seven of them—occurred between 1995 and 2000, four suffered by Terry Bowden and three by Tuberville, with two in 2000 alone, including the SEC Championship Game.

4) South Carolina still has not beaten Auburn since joining the SEC. Brad Scott coached the Gamecocks in losses to Dameyune Craig-led squads in 1996 and 1997, and Spurrier has now dropped three to the Tigers. If only we'd gotten a shot at one of Lou Holtz's squads, too...

5) South Carolina state champions! And that's worth... um... something. Yeah.

* Other assorted thoughts as your humble Wishbone duo watched the **South Carolina Shakedown**:

Van: Dyer started the game making me think, "Wow—Lattimore is so much better than Dyer at this point in their careers." By the end, I was thinking, "Wow—Dyer is awesome and Lattimore is not impressing me!' Dyer just gets stronger as the game goes on. And he plays "bigger" as the game goes on. He starts the game looking like Markeith "the Lizard" Cooper and ends the game looking like Rudi Johnson. That's astonishing.

John: South Carolina was the highest ranked team we will play until we play Alabama. And we won. Our offense was awesome. The USC defense is good and we rolled up and down the field for long drives on them. Dyer was feeling it in the second half and dragging tacklers. Newton threw to the other receivers—Blake, Lutzenkirchen, Eric Smith, etc. The defense did just enough. And Spurrier was his own worst enemy. I was much more scared of Garcia coming back into the game than some freshman. In our stadium, at night, losing in a tight SEC game, you throw in a freshman QB???? It smacked of desperation—or of the old Spurrier quarterback yo-yo. Stupid.

Van: Yeah, I'm just gonna stick my backup rookie QB in the game in the fourth quarter with the game on the line. What's the worst that could happen? And wouldn't it have been funny if Jesse Palmer had been doing the color commentary?

John: Josh Bynes is a man. I love our freshman defensive linemen, Whitaker and Lemonior. And the best two players on special teams are freshmen defensive players - Craig Sanders (DE) and Demetruce McNeal (safety).

Van: How do you feel about Mario Fannin at this point?

John: I like him as a player and I am glad that he is on our football team. But I would prefer that we not hand him the ball in an SEC game again, ever. If we want to throw him a few passes out of the slot and have him fall down or get out of bounds immediately after catching the ball, I can live with that, but nothing more.

Van: I was so wrung out by the time of the last interception to seal the win, I couldn't even get all that excited. I spent the whole game pacing and fretting and jumping up and down, and finally all I could do was sit there and feel numb. But it was a good kind of numb—the kind of numb that comes from winning a slugfest and seeing the other guy lying there on the mat instead of you. You're swaying and you're bleeding, but at least you're the one still standing.

John: South Carolina can win the East if Spurrier doesn't torpedo them with this quarterback thing. Bring on LA-Monroe and give every Auburn fan's heart and fingernails a week off.

Van: There was a moment in the broadcast of the game Saturday night when the offense was clicking along toward an imminent touchdown and running something like a play every twenty seconds—and the camera zoomed in on Gamecocks Defensive

Coordinator Ellis Johnson in the press box, and his eyes were about as big around as dinner plates. You have to love it when a plan comes together.

And speaking of the offense clicking along—don't you think Pat Dye was smiling as he watched that offense grind out the yards, run play after run play, scarcely ever putting the ball in the air, just imposing our will on the SC defense? The Tigers may not have been lined up in the eponymous wishbone, but they almost seemed to be running some kind of "triple option" attack as Cam pitched it, handed it off, or kept it himself. He looked like Randy Campbell out there (with a few more inches of height and an extra hundred pounds of muscle)!

And while we're on the subjects of South Carolina and Steve Spurrier, am I the only person who has ever noticed that Auburn's 2005 win over South Carolina was by the exact same score, 48-7, as the beatdown Spurrier inflicted on Pat Dye's 1990 squad in his first season at Florida? That fact continues to make me happy—I was in attendance at both games and was extremely aware of it. I've always wondered if Tommy Tuberville realized it—or if Pat Dye ever noticed it.

And one more item before we leave the Palmetto State in the rear view at last: It's neat that South Carolina's band plays both their famous "2001: A Space Odyssey" and the theme from the original (David Lynch) "Dune" movie during games. It's like a medley of the hits from the most pretentious and tedious Sci Fi movies ever made. (Gamecocks gather around the "Monolith" that is Spurrier's ego, maybe? Someone throws a chicken drumstick bone in the air in slow motion, whereupon it turns into the Goodyear Blimp? He who controls the game clock controls the universe?) Then again, we probably shouldn't make too much fun. After all, the Auburn band famously plays the "Imperial March" from the Star Wars movies-- otherwise known as the theme song of the guys that got beaten by Ewoks.

And lastly, this week's **Wishbone SEC Power Rankings**:

The Elite: Alabama. We're torn between wanting them to lose immediately vs. wanting them to be undefeated so we can possibly by some miracle ruin their season.

The Very Good: Auburn, LSU, Florida, Arkansas, South Carolina. A fine jumble of very good teams here at the second tier, with the Pork Products and Hot Wings dropping to the bottom two spots following losses. The thinking here, though, is that neither of them will lose many more the rest of the way. As for Florida—who knows? I guess we'll find out more soon enough.

The "Might Be Good": Kentucky. Ditto the Florida point above. See you soon in Lexington!

The Not Good: Tennessee, Miss. State, Georgia, Vanderbilt. And let's be honest: If Georgia played Vandy tomorrow, how quick would you *really* be to take the Dawgs?

The Wretched: Ole Miss. But, hey—a win is a win, right?

The Wishbone will be reuniting in Lexington for the Kentucky game. Perhaps the aura of our combined presence in the stadium will be just enough to pull the Tigers through. And maybe we'll get a photo together for the first time since the early Clinton administration...

As it turned out, the Wishbone duo did not get to reunite at the Kentucky game, as circumstances conspired to prevent John from traveling to Lexington.

Van, however, did make the trip, visiting one of the last two SEC venues he'd never previously been to for an Auburn game. (The other remains Arkansas.) And what a great time was had by the Plexicos. The Kentucky fans were hospitable, generous, and polite— more so than any other fan base Van had ever experienced.

The game, of course, turned out to be anything but pleasant— particularly late. Auburn during the first quarter had threatened to blow things out, but the offense slowed down and the defense began giving up scores and the next thing anyone knew, the Wildcats had drawn even and threatened to win.

Such a turn of events was not entirely improbable; after all, Kentucky had beaten the Tigers in Jordan-Hare the previous season, for the first time in the living memory of either of your intrepid Wishbone columnists. Throw in the fact that the last road game Van had attended was the 2008 Vanderbilt game—the first time Auburn had lost to that foe in decades—and the omens appeared quite negative.

But then Cam took the game into his hands and began to reveal to everyone that he was a force to be reckoned with—a force that simply would not be denied...

– KENTUCKY WEEK –

Take a Deep Breath, Tigers...!

"It's the deep breath before the plunge."
--Gandalf, Lord of the Rings: Return of the King

And so the Cam-not-running aberration known as "the Louisiana-Monroe game" is behind us now. For that matter, believe it or not, nearly half the season is behind us. Once again, we stand at 5-0. Once again, we await with breathless anticipation the three-game mid-season endurance contest that will surely define the year for us: Kentucky-Arkansas-LSU.

Using the terms of GOL TV's great analyst, Ray Hudson, the remainder of the schedule will begin asking Auburn a series of very probing questions over the following weeks, and the answers the Tigers are able to provide will go a long way toward determining the way we feel when we look back at this season in the years to come.

But that is for tomorrow. For today, as we bask in the afterglow of the stress-free weekend-that-was, the Wishbone finds itself free to ponder deeper and broader cosmic questions.

* Where Does This Year's Team Stand Relative to Last Year (and Beyond)?

Fans and the media always talk about "bend but don't break" defenses but you rarely see as clear an example of the phenomenon as the 2010 Auburn defense. The Tigers have given up only two pass plays over fifty yards this season, but are only 89th in the nation in pass defense at 280 yards per game. How can this be? Short passes. A *lot* of short passes.

Tell us something we don't know, though, right? How about this: Even given the disturbing state of the short-range pass coverage, Auburn's defense is ranked a lofty twelfth in the nation (and *second* in the SEC!) in *rushing* defense. The Tigers are allowing an average of only 86 measly yards per game on the ground, or a paltry 2.64 yards per carry. By way of contrast, Auburn allowed 153 rushing yards per game through this point in 2009, placing the Tigers 89th in the nation and near the bottom of the SEC.

Okay, so Auburn's defense can stop the run and doesn't give up big passing plays. So teams are taking what works for them: the short passing game. Lamentable as it may be that our proud defense is lax at any one thing, the silver lining here is that the Tigers are forcing teams to drive down the field in five-yard chunks—tough to do without a penalty or a dropped pass, or without Nick Fairley blowing up a play or two (or a quarterback or two) and ending the drive.

At this point in 2009 the Tigers led the SEC in only two categories: turnover margin and sacks allowed. (And by the end of the season, they had fallen deep into the middle of the national pack in both areas.) This season, Auburn leads the SEC in *four* categories (the same number as Alabama)—rushing offense, total offense, passing efficiency and tackles for loss. What's more, the passing efficiency number is tops *nationally*. We can move the ball. We can run it (with multiple backs finding success) and we can throw it (even deep, if we need to).

And we have that X-factor that can kick in when things appear hopeless: CamZilla. When was the last time Auburn had an X-factor at quarterback that could pull out a flamboyant and dramatic run or deep pass when we absolutely had to have it? Jason Campbell in 2004, we'd argue—when all else failed, ol' Number 17 could uncork a bomb to Ace (Aromashodu) or Deuce (Obomanu) or one of the others and pull our collective bacon out of the fire. That brace of wideouts we so took for granted, that left us after 2005 (taking

Brandon Cox's passing numbers with them), has at last been replaced by a new monster squad that keeps showing flashes of immense potential and phenomenal brilliance.

In sum, while the Tigers may be allowing the short pass to yield a few more yards than most of us would like, the "bend but don't break" defense is forcing the opposition to *earn* every one of those yards and, what is more, not allowing them to do it the old-fashioned, will-asserting, manly way—on the ground. Meanwhile, the offense can run the ball (like a steamroller!) and even pass it with tremendous efficiency. Yes, as the old maxim says we should do, *we are running* and *we are stopping the run*. And we're no slouches at passing it, either. And that, my friends, traditionally leads to good things. Very good things.

* Crazy Like a Fox? Or Crazy Like a Rabid Fox?

Les Miles is fortunate that college football coaching does not require a license. If it did, said license would surely have been suspended by now. Or outright revoked.

There have been clever and tricky coaches for as long as there have been coaches in general—for as long as football has existed. For every "show them you're man enough and grind it out" guy, there's another who would rather show you how smart he is—or how dumb you are, for falling for it. We're talking the tricksters, the gamblers, the dice-rollers extraordinaire. College football has always been filled with this sort of person; an array of head coaches who seem to relish the "gotcha" moment more than an actual victory. And yet, at their core, nearly every coach has at least some basic understanding of the fundamentals of the sport—a sense of when to do what, and when not to do what.

Yes, there are gamblers and risk-takers. And then there's that other category, a category reserved for the tiny minority who is the *beyond*-gambler, the *beyond*-risk taker. Here we're talking the coach who is simply flat-out, bat-$#*t *crazy*.

And that brings us to Les Miles.

In attempting to describe to a casual college football fan just how crazy Les Miles truly is, one of your intrepid Wishbone duo actually had to resort to drawing a graph. We have recreated it here, in all its nutty glory: The *Scale of College Football Coaching Craziness* ™.

This scale ranges from the "Ultra-Conservative" to basically "Conservative," to "Getting Tricky," to outright "Gamblers," to "Les Miles."

Ultra Conservative   Conservative   Tricky   Gamblers   Les M.

Now, for illustrative purposes, let us place a few well-known coaches onto this spectrum:

The Ultra-Conservative
An ideal series of downs for the Ultra-Conservative features three runs, mostly up the middle, generating the requisite "clouds of dust," and with no trick plays ever—heavens, we'd rather forfeit than resort to *that!*—and almost no passing. For the Ultra-Conservative, the ideal player is the fullback, and the preferred term for his players is "hard-nosed." Examples of this species include old-school types such as Woody Hayes, Bo Schembechler, and Jackie Sherrill.

The Conservative
One of the favored quotes of this species is, "Only three things can happen when you throw the ball, and two of them are bad." Don't take too many risks. Run the ball and play defense. If it's late in the game and you're trailing and it's fourth down, go ahead and punt—you know your defense will give you the ball back in time for one more shot at a score. Examples include Pat Dye, Mack Brown, Nick Saban, and even our beloved former Coach Tubs, who found himself acquiring a "Gambler" reputation but in his heart was always a Conservative.

Getting Tricky
The Tricky Boys are willing to fully embrace a riskier offense, and trick plays are fine as part of that scheme. Even so, there's still a very sound, fundamental approach at work just beneath that flashy surface. Often they resort to the trickiness in order to compensate for a perceived drop-off in talent between their players and the opposition; ironically, they then win games, get better jobs at schools with better players on hand, and consequently end up resorting to the trickiness less and less. Coaches who like to Get

Tricky include Urban Meyer and new Notre Dame boss Chip Kelly, and Bobby Bowden had his moments utilizing this philosophy over the years, as well. Tuberville started out here, but you could just see the relief on his face once he built up the Auburn talent level to the point that he felt he could embrace his inner Conservative.

The Gambler

The Gambler is a gambler for one of two reasons: because he feels that he has to be, or because he just gets off on it. The first variety of Gambler probably coaches at a mid-major program, or else at a low-end program in a bigger conference. He looks around and sees the talent deficit he's saddled with and he says, "Boys, we can make up this here difference by out-thinking and out-surprising the (likely Conservative) coach and players of that there big-time program we're playing this week!" Sometimes it even works. The second variety of Gambler is just a tick or two above Les Miles Land. He possibly suffers from some undiagnosed mental imbalance that leads him to want to not only win, but win all complicated-ly and fancy-like. He talks about concepts such as "basketball on grass" and "surgery with a chainsaw." In either case, he will call any play at any time in the game. Onside kick to start the game? Flea-flicker? Statue of Liberty? Fake punt? Go for it on fourth down on your own side of the field, early in the game? No problem! Let's do it all! Twice each! Coaches who have exhibited some form of this behavior include Chris Peterson, Rich Rodriguez, Hal Mumme, and Mike Leach.

The Les Miles

Les Miles (let's be honest—the name "Mad Hatter" no longer seems quite crazy enough for him) has transcended all of the above categories and has become a category unto himself. The Les Miles coach is endlessly inventive in his jaw-dropping, mind-numbing counter-intuitive-ness: Go for it on fourth down multiple times late in a big-time conference game, when you have one of the best defenses in the country? Why not! Call a pass play when you're down just a point or two and there's probably only time for one play left and you're easily within field goal range? What the heck! And the *Pièce de résistance*: You're down four points and on the opponent's goal line, with no timeouts and the clock ticking below fifteen seconds—so you send in the substitutes! It confuses the defense and draws a "too many men on the field" penalty, thus allowing you to overcome the implosion of your offense that you somehow just *knew* was about to happen.

Fortunately for the *Les Miles* coach, the sheer craziness of this coaching style in some inexplicable way actually appears to warp the space-time continuum and cause the very laws of nature and of probability to skew dramatically awry. How else to explain the way so many *Les Miles*-ish decisions actually *work*?

(To be fair, though—do they *really and truly* "work?" In this particular example, the panicked LSU subs so discombobulated Tennessee that their defense ended up with not just twelve but thirteen men on the field during the aforementioned offensive screw-up. The whole affair was so risky, so chaotic, and so mind-numbingly stupid that it actually caused the other team to mess up, probably from the sheer shock of it all. But note to all the Les Miles coaches out there—and if there's a God in Heaven, there aren't that many of them—being so inept that the other team is sucked into a penalty because of your ineptness is *not* the same thing as having a "brilliant plan" actually succeed.)

But, hey—living your life the Les Miles way has its advantages, we suppose. There's danger, excitement, and the disbelieving stares of those close to you. (In this case, some 92,000 close to him.) If you would like to live life on the edge and try this approach for yourself, all you have to do is visit the iTunes store and download the "Miles Method" app!

So many jokes, so many jokes... As the battery runs low, does it panic and begin erasing your music files? But we think the app speaks for itself. (We just would not believe anything it actually says.)

This Week's Wishbone SEC Power Rankings, Express Edition

The Elite
Alabama. Ye Gods. We think Amorak Huey said it best this week: *We want them to think they're invincible when we play them...* but they might actually *be*.

The Very Good

Auburn, South Carolina, Arkansas, LSU. With a more sane coach, would LSU have won the Tennessee game in a bigger way... or would they have *lost* it, because they didn't do the "Meltdown on Fourth Down?"

The Might Be Good
Florida, Kentucky. The question for Florida is how quickly they can recover from that emasculation in Tuscaloosa. Those other guys in blue there, we'll find out how good they are in a few days.

The Not Good
Georgia, Ole Miss, Miss. State, Tennessee. But, hey, congrats to the Rebels for moving up to "Not Good" this week.

The Wretched
Vanderbilt. Welcome home, Dores. This category was missing you.

*What Kentucky **should** have done after the game...*

49

If South Carolina week brought with it a sense of a likely loss, Arkansas week stalked in like the Grim Reaper, his scythe set to slash down Auburn's hopes and dreams.

Why wouldn't it feel that way? How many previous seasons had felt so good, so right...only to see the Hawgs rush in and trample our SEC and national championship chances under their mighty... um... pigs' feet?

And that got John and Van to thinking—do the Hawgs actually have some sort of hex over Auburn? And if they do, just how bad has it been—and how can we get rid of the thing?

And that brings us to "The Hawg Hex—and How to Break it..." Incidentally, this was also our first column to get widespread link-age on other sports sites across the Internet, which was gratifying and made us feel like maybe somebody was reading this stuff!

The Hawg Hex – and How to Break It

Part 1: The Hex

The history of the Auburn-Arkansas rivalry is not a long one, like Auburn-Georgia, nor is it studded with bizarre oddities like the Auburn-LSU series. But it *is* one fraught with more than its share of upsets and shocking outcomes, not to mention season-wrecking derailings (or season-derailing wrecks!) that knocked Auburn out of SEC Championship Game appearances and bigger bowl berths.

So, before we break down this year's matchup and look at what Auburn has learned (or should have learned) about itself up to this point in the season, let's look back at the brief but electrically charged history of Tigers vs. Hawgs.

We begin with the first clash between the two, when Arkansas was still a member of the oft-not-lamented Southwestern Conference. All that stands out in the collective memory of your intrepid columnists about that 1984 Liberty Bowl tilt was Auburn's wishbone attack facing Arkansas' then-newfangled "flexbone" offense. Suffice to say the good guys won, even with Bo Jackson sidelined with an injury. No hex detected as of yet.

Once Arkansas entered the SEC in 1992, however, an astute observer could already sniff the beginnings of what we will refer to as the "Hawg Hex" in the air. That 24-24 draw in Jordan-Hare denied Pat Dye a winning record and possibly a bowl berth in his final season. The following year, when Terry Bowden's first squad traveled to Fayetteville for the first time in Auburn history, they had to wait while tractors scraped snow and ice off the field, even as AU equipment guys raided local stores for heavy winter gear they hadn't known they'd need to bring. Clearly, this was a sign of Hell freezing over, as Auburn actually managed to defeat Arkansas 31-21 in a season where doing so made a difference.*

The next clash of note came in 1995, and with this game the Hawg Hex was in full effect. Had Auburn prevailed, they would have won the SEC West Division and played in their first SEC Championship Game. Arkansas led 30-20 with time winding down until Pat Nix engineered a scoring drive (and two-point conversion) to pull the score to 30-28. Getting the ball back, Auburn drove into field goal position and Matt Hawkins lined up to win the game on the final play.

Of course, he missed. The Hex had struck again. Heck, even the sporting gods frowned on this game—its climactic moments occurred just as the Atlanta Braves were recording the final outs of the decisive game of their only World Series victory on another channel, so the viewing audience was probably exceptionally low.

The 1999 game is just a blur in the Wishbone's memory. Amid much media hype that Tommy Tuberville was leading his first Auburn team to his home state, the Tigers laid an immense egg in Fayetteville against a mediocre Hawgs squad, losing 34-10 in a contest that wasn't even that close. Certainly other games that season were much more winnable—crushing last-second losses at home to Ole Miss and Mississippi State spring to mind—but a win at Arkansas would have given Tuberville a winning record and likely put the Tigers in a bowl game. With the loss, Auburn would end the season 5-6 and home for the holidays.

The Hawg Hex bloomed into full, unquestionable, awful intensity in the back-to-back thrashings of 2001 and 2002. In the 2001 contest, Auburn held things close until a series of unfortunate events, mostly orchestrated by running quarterback (and perpetual thorn-in-AU's-side) Matt Jones, led to a runaway 42-17 victory in

Fayetteville. The following year, in Jordan-Hare, Jones was joined in the mayhem by the seemingly untackleable Fred Talley at running back (ahh, the miserable history of Auburn defenses facing the scrawny scat-backs!), pacing the Hawgs to a 38-17 win. ** (There is a generation of young Auburn fans whose parents threaten, "Do your chores—or else Fred Talley will run loose on you!") In both of those seasons, an Auburn victory would have put the Tigers in the SEC Championship Game. In both of those seasons, Arkansas came from nowhere to administer unholy beat-downs to the Tigers.

Of course, when it comes to knocking Auburn out of bigger things, the 2006 Arkansas game probably retires the trophy. Auburn fans almost seem to forget that the Tigers achieved 11 victories that season (including a delicious bowl win over Nebraska that should be savored greatly)—an accomplishment equaled or exceeded by only few the greatest squads in modern AU history. And yet, for all of that, the Tigers' loss to Arkansas spoiled the picture because it knocked Auburn out of contention for conference and perhaps national honors. A win over Arkansas that day ultimately would have given Auburn the SEC Western Division title and a berth in the SEC Championship Game against the about-to-be 2006 National Champion Florida Gators—a team the Tigers had already beaten that season. After the opening kickoff, however, the fact that the day would belong to Arkansas was never in doubt. The Hawgs won 27-10 in a contest that wasn't as close as the score indicates. Then-Hawg OC Gus Malzahn (why is that name familiar?) impressed observers by pulling out all the stops in a trick-play fiesta that left Auburn's defensive players dazed and confused (and at least one Wishbone writer wistfully dreaming that Gus might someday become Auburn's offensive coordinator).

The 2008 game pitted first-year Razorbacks Coach Bobby Petrino against his former boss, Tommy Tuberville, in what would turn out to be the latter's final season. This Hawg squad was considered poor at best and would go on to finish with a 5-7 record. Even so, they managed a 25-22 victory that condemned the Tigers to a losing record, prevented them from reaching six wins, and likely knocked them out of a bowl appearance. Two months later, Tuberville was out and Petrino was being hailed as one of the brightest coaches in the SEC. So goes the Hawg Hex.

Before someone points it out—yes, we do understand that in most of those years, it wasn't *just* the loss to Arkansas that did the Tigers in; yes, a win over some *other* team would have given Auburn the requisite number of wins instead. But the point is, in most of those years, the "other" teams were the Floridas and LSUs and Alabamas. Arkansas is not a *bad* program, but they're not Florida or LSU or Alabama. They are a team that most Auburn fans reasonably believe we should defeat more often than not. And while we do manage at least occasional (but decreasingly frequent) wins over them,*** we seem to lose to them far more often than we should, and at the most inopportune of moments, to boot. The overall record currently sits at 10-8-1 in Auburn's favor. Only a narrow, hanging-on-at-the-last-second 2-point win in 2007 stands between us and a dead-even series, with Arkansas taking the last *four*. Thus: The Hawg Hex.

So: In the words of Lenin, what is to be done? What can we take from this season's performances by each team that gives us some indication of what's going to happen on Saturday, and what the Tigers can and should do to increase their chances of pulling out the critical victory?

Part 2: How to Break the Hex

Let's look first at Auburn and how we got to where we are today: sitting first in the SEC West at 6-0.

The Tigers have played four BCS-level teams and two cupcakes. Of the four BCS-level games, Auburn won three of them by a field goal each, and the fourth by eight points.

The reasons why those games were as close as they were are legion and have been well-documented. Each one featured a different dysfunction somewhere along the way, whether it be failing to show up for at least one quarter (or half!), turning the ball over at inopportune moments, failing to *create* turnovers by the opponent when they would do the most good, giving up vast tracts of real estate to short-passing attacks, and so on.

Why are we 6-0 despite these issues? It's obvious: the X-factor at quarterback is (so far) a magic eraser capable of wiping away all that bad juju almost singlehandedly. *Just*. Thus, four very close wins from games in which either the offense or defense or both

54

appeared to check out of the game for at least a quarter. (In retrospect, the offseason mantra of "Good to Great" could have effectively been shortened to "Sign Cam.")

Arkansas, meanwhile, has looked impressive even against very good teams—and everyone knows how they performed against Alabama. Their defense is much improved (from a defense that, a year ago, was still perfectly capable of shutting down Auburn's offense for much of that game). The quarterback is arguably the best passer in the conference and will be facing a pass defense allowing 65% of opponents' passes to be completed—a defense for which the word "porous" might actually be a compliment.

This is, of course, somewhat by design, due to Ted Roof's schemes favoring stopping the run and the long pass—though surely the expectation was for a lower short-pass-completion percentage than *that*. (While simulating this game on X-Box, the in-game AI actually admonished Auburn-coaching Ringer for playing an unsound pass defense!) No one believes that Auburn is going to suddenly change defensive philosophies mid-season, so a reasonable expectation would be for a lot of Hawg receivers to catch the ball on Saturday and for the Tigers to surrender mucho yardage via the air.

So is the defensive side of the equation hopeless? Not quite. We believe Auburn can salvage this situation in three ways:

1: Tackle better when opponents catch the ball. Auburn has gone from being one of the better-tackling teams in college football five or six years ago to one of the worst now. We've seen far too many missed tackles, too many defensive players diving at ankles and missing, in the past month.

2: Get pressure on Ryan Mallet. Mr. Fairley and Mr. Carter need to do Saturday what they were never able to do against Mike Hartline in Lexington: arrive at the quarterback while he still has the ball and rudely introduce him to the turf. Mallett is not the same type of quarterback as Hartline, who skips around and zips the ball out of there in something like one-and-a-half seconds every play. Mallett can be gotten-to. He's hard to bring down and he has a quick release, but Auburn needs to at least make him uncomfortable back there and throw off the timing of the Petrino offense. Can it be done? We think so. Arkansas has not faced a defensive line like Auburn's yet. (But they played Alabama, you argue. Guess what? The Tide is last in the SEC in sacks. Believe it or not, Kentucky has almost twice as many sacks as Alabama.)

3: Generate long, sustained drives on offense. If you watched the Alabama comeback against the Hawgs, the Tide seemed to go mostly with the wildcat formation in the second half and Arkansas had a hard time stopping the run later in the game. Auburn needs to keep running the ball—and not just with Cam carrying it—to wear down the Hawg defense. We have already seen this season that while Dr. Gustav prefers the "pedal to the metal" approach on offense, he's fully capable of slowing things down and grinding it out and running the clock (the Soul-Crushing Drive against Kentucky was the latest example), and this is probably what we will need to do during at least part of the game this week.

Taking the games each has played against its three strongest opponents, we find that Auburn's scoring differential (4.6) is only marginally ahead of Arkansas's (3.3). Halfway through the season, remarkably, the only common opponent they have shared so far is Louisiana-Monroe; both the Tigers and the Hawgs held the War Hawks to a single score, with Auburn running up 52 points to Arkansas' 31. Ryan Mallett threw for four hundred yards and three touchdowns in that affair, while Cam threw for 245 and three TDs. What can we learn from that? Not much really. We're terribly, terribly in the dark going into this game.

What *do* we know? As Coach Chizik might put it, "Auburn has learned how to win close games." (The Wishbone adds, "And also learned how to give us all heart attacks on a weekly basis.") Arkansas, meanwhile, has shown the ability to *lose* close games—or at least one close game. But we honestly don't have enough evidence to go on, beyond that. Arkansas' defense is better than last year, but Auburn's offense is better, too. The Hex aside, trends point toward another close game, and we can only hope that prevailing in such contests truly is a "learned" skill.

Any other reasons for optimism? Any other signs that the dreaded Hawg Hex might be broken, at least this year? Here are three more small reasons for optimism:

1: As much as Auburn gets flagged for this and that (often seemingly imaginary) violation, Arkansas is actually the most penalized team in the SEC. It would be nice to watch a game in which Auburn is the *least*-penalized team on the field for a change. Perhaps this will be the week.

2: Arkansas is 11th in the SEC in turnover margin, including giving up a surprising *seven* interceptions. Despite Auburn's difficulties of late in generating turnovers, this is another micro-trend that might benefit the home team.

3: While Auburn has seemed to pick random *quarters* to not play well, Arkansas overall has been a first *half* team. They did not score a second half touchdown in their last two games and they have been outscored in the fourth quarter for the season. Meanwhile Auburn has outscored its opponents in every quarter, but the Tigers are at their best in the *fourth*, where they are outscoring opponents 41-13. What does that means for Saturday? Expect Arkansas to jump ahead early, then turn the ball over a time or two, and finally see Auburn come from behind and give us yet another nail biter.

In sum: while the Hawg Hex is malevolent and mighty, it may not be strong enough to slow down CamZilla. The *X-factor*, we believe, may be just enough to overcome the *Hex factor*.

Whatever happens on Saturday, just remember—regardless of the result, come next week we'll have seven whole days to talk about Les Miles.

* The 1993 Auburn win over Arkansas *did* make a difference in terms of preserving an undefeated Auburn streak that would ultimately reach twenty games the next year. Conversely, however, one might well argue that because the Tigers were on probation, they had nothing *tangible* (bowl berths; SEC title game appearances) on the line to lose anyway.

** The orange t-shirt Van wore to the 2002 Auburn-Arkansas game (at the behest of Tommy Tuberville and his "all orange" campaign) was the same shirt Van wore to the 2001 Iron Bowl—and we all remember what happened there. Those were the only two games to which that shirt was ever worn. Suffice to say, it has never seen the light of day again.

*** The 2000, 2003, and 2004 games deserve special mention because, while Auburn prevailed in each of them, the Hex still lingered in the background and made its presence felt at times. The outcome of the 2000 contest was in doubt till the final whistle and a late (intentional) safety by Auburn—reflecting how desperate the Tigers were to get the thing over with—brought the final margin to only 21-19. The 2003 Auburn victory, 10-3, was largely due to holding calls nullifying long scoring runs by Matt Jones and one of the backs. And in 2004, Arkansas (of all opponents!) scored more points—20—against the eventual Sugar Bowl Champs than any other team the Tigers faced in the regular season.

Given the remarkable number of close games and come-from-behind victories by the Tigers in 2010—and especially what happened in the Iron Bowl, about which more later, obviously—it's hard to say that one game in the middle of the season might eventually be the one we all look back on as the key win of the season. And even if we do allow that as a possibility, surely it would be the LSU game—that titanic clash of SEC West undefeateds, won by only a single late score—that would qualify for that honor.

To the contrary, argue the Wishbone columnists. As we gaze back upon the season (and especially the middle of the season), the game that stands out to us as the most remarkable and perhaps vital in helping the Tigers reach their goals was the Arkansas game.

The outcome of that contest was in doubt until very late. The Auburn defense showed very few signs of ever being able to stop the Arkansas offense consistently, even after quarterback Ryan Mallet was injured and was replaced by his understudy (perhaps especially after that happened!).

The Razorbacks were more or less holding serve with the Tigers until late in the fourth quarter, when a sudden string of events resulted in Auburn running away to a 65-43 win.

Beating a team like Arkansas, which would go on to defeat LSU and secure a spot in the Sugar Bowl, after giving up 43 points to them—it's almost inconceivable.

This was the week when we all realized that it almost didn't matter how poorly Auburn's defense played, because somehow, some way, Cam and his supporting cast on offense would always be able to find a way to overcome that adversity and simply outscore the opponent.

The one caveat to that, of course, was, "What if the opponent has the best defense in the conference, and actually manages to limit Auburn's offense to only a relatively few points?" That very question is the one we faced the very next week, as the Bayou Bengals came to town.

Another one lurked just behind it, though—a question predicated on the knowledge that one single player was making so much of a difference for the Tigers. And that was the question the Wishbone addressed first in that next week's column...

Everything You Wanted in an LSU Column—and Les!

Thoughts on This Auburn Team, Right Now:

We all know the truth by now. We don't exactly speak of it openly, but the fact is there, in plain sight—it's the 260 pound quarterback in the room. And that truth is this: As long as Cameron Newton remains healthy, Auburn has a chance to win every game on the schedule—and perhaps one or two *not* currently on the schedule. But if something horrific and unthinkable should befall him... we basically become last year's squad, minus Ben Tate; or the 1999 team, with Barrett Trotter starring in the role of Ben Leard, and Darvin Adams as Ronney Daniels, and a much weaker defense. Ack.

So let's all just metaphorically gather 'round and say a prayer to the deity (or lack thereof) of our choice, shall we? Because, Cam— we need ya, pal. In a way that few teams have *ever* needed that one guy before, we need ya. Even the early-1980s teams that featured game-changing Bo Jackson had a fantastic defense they could rely upon, more often than not. Rarely did those squads have to get into a track meet and essentially *outscore* someone (the 1984 and 85 Florida State games notwithstanding). In Pat Dye's world, such a thought was virtually anathema.

Even as Cam's personal rushing stats have increased, the rest of the rushing game has regressed. Dyer is hobbled—just as we arrive at crunch time, no less. Fannin continues to fumble (and surely can't count on another howler of a call from the replay booth for the rest of the season). For the most part, and especially against a fast defense, McCalebb is useful for one thing only, aside from last weekend's superlative kick return: being the decoy on the "jet sweep." By the coaches' own admission, you dare not run him up the gut like a "true" running back. He's an "edge" guy. He doesn't even catch passes, *a la* Fannin—at least, not yet. And what about tough-as-nails Eric Smith? Fabulous blocker, sure; but, to our knowledge, he's carried the ball in a meaningful situation precisely *once* this season, and got stuffed for no gain.

So Cam is no longer just the X-Factor we've been calling him here. He's now seemingly *the entire running game*, at least until Dyer gets healthy again.

Talk about putting all your eggs (or footballs, or fortunes) in one basket. Good heavens. Please stay healthy, Cam. Please.

What if they Held a Track Meet and Called it a Football Game?

A track meet? The proper analogy is probably a tennis match. For the better part of three-plus quarters in the defensive coordinators' Purgatory that was Auburn vs. Arkansas, it looked for all the world like the team that could hold serve and break the other's serve would win—and ultimately that's what happened. (Both teams' defenses were essentially the net—the ball sailed over and past it, and even *through* it, with ease.) The famous Arkansas fumble and return for a touchdown was the "service breaker" that put Auburn ahead by more than a single score, and from there Arkansas was forced into (or Petrino chose to go with) trying for booming "aces" on his serves, rather than sticking with "serve and volley." And in doing so, he double-faulted. Twice. Game, set, match.

And who among us who watched tennis during the great McEnroe/Borg/Connors era can think of that sport without thinking of the controversial calls by the referees (and the subsequent outcries by spectators and fans) that seemed to define the time? Which brings us, very reluctantly but necessarily, to the officials and their multiple "ruling on the field is upheld" moments from Saturday.

Fannin fumbled. Yes, we all know he fumbled. We were not even surprised that it happened, to be honest. It was Fannin, after all. We love him as a blocker and a receiver out of the backfield, but when he's handed the ball and told to dive into the scrum... well, the throat gets a tad constricted and we start having trouble breathing and we break out in hives. So, yeah, Hawgs fans—you got hosed on that one. No argument here.

Which just about made up for the phantom holding call on Auburn's first drive and phantom pass interference call on Arkansas' second drive.

So, yeah, that's that. As for the rest of the non-overturns: Forget it. You guys know as well as we do that there has to be "indisputable visual evidence" in order to overturn the call on the field. That's the rule. Asking the refs to overturn a call you don't like, when none of the camera angles actually *shows* what you want to see or backs up what you believe, is bogus. You may be perfectly sure in your heart that something happened a certain way, but if the replay doesn't actually *show* it, there is no "indisputable visual evidence." Blame CBS for their choices of camera placement, if you want, but don't blame the refs for actually following the rules. End of story.

The BCS and Related BS

Speaking of the BCS, we of the Wishbone have differing views that have festered into an open clash this week. We present for you here our open disagreement, for you the esteemed reader to absorb and to judge:

John: There are many kinds of Auburn fans. This week there are two distinct types of Auburn fans - those that want to look ahead and think about what might be and those that do not. Van is a great example of the "looking ahead" Auburn fan - he sat down Sunday morning and started browsing SEC Championship Game tickets online. Then, after the BCS rankings came out, he started checking out BCS title game tickets. [*It's true. —Van*] He is already very worried that Auburn might get *"2004ed"* again. (We are trademarking the term *"2004ed"* right now—and hoping we never, ever have to use it in reference to Auburn.)

I am the other kind of Auburn fan right now. I don't want to look ahead at all. Partly because we are playing a Top Ten team this week—a team that crushed us last season—but also because after what happened in 2004 I just want to live in the moment and enjoy my team. I enjoyed that great roller coaster ride of a game on Saturday, but I did not immediately start scoreboard-watching the other Top Ten teams.

I also want to point out that for those of us who prefer defense-oriented teams over offense-oriented ones, this year's Auburn team is fun but sometimes painful to watch. It is like a great ice cream sundae after a topping you don't like has been added. I love defense. 2004? Great defense. 1988? My favorite Auburn defense ever. There's no play I enjoy seeing more than a great quarterback sack. And so watching this year's defense get carved up, week after week, is very hard to stomach. I am not complaining and I am delighted that we have Malzahn and Cam and this offense and we are winning... but, for a defense-minded fan, it is still not easy.

Van: It's true. I'll admit it. I am looking ahead and thinking ahead. I wasn't doing so egregiously until maybe after the South Carolina game—a game I was certain beforehand that we would lose. Then came Arkansas, another matchup (not to mention a certain "Hex") I felt spelled certain doom for us. Somehow, we won both games— and at almost the same time, a certain formerly imposing team from across the state started looking remarkably human and vulnerable.

So now I'm almost, *almost*, buying into the whole "team of destiny" hype. Me, an Auburn Man—the same guy who berated John endlessly in 2004 with the grim prophecy, "John, Southern Cal and Oklahoma are *not* going to lose, because we are Auburn and that is what happens to us." That guy, that ultra-realistic guy, is buying into the hype. Good lord. It has come to this.

But I just can't help it. After the "should have beens" like 1983 and 2004, and the "if not fors" like 1993, and the "so stinkin' closes" like 1988 and 2006, I'm not just hungry for a championship...I'm not just *starving* for one... I'm freaking RAVENOUS for one. The only year I actually bought into the hype before the season even started was 2003, and we all remember how that worked out. (Look for my column on that very topic coming up in the offseason.) So I try very hard to keep my expectations under control and to a minimum. But, on the other hand, when seasons like this one suddenly bloom into reality, I say let's enjoy it while we can. I'm pretty confident I don't have any cosmic super ability to affect the outcome of the remaining games, no matter what John may think, so all of my looking ahead and shopping for bowl tickets and generally reveling in this brief shining moment can't possibly have any negative repercussions for the team. Right? *Right??*

John: I also don't want to look ahead because we are playing LSU and crazy Les Miles this week and they are plenty good enough to beat Auburn on Saturday. So don't stress about Oregon and Oklahoma and Boise State and the Harris Poll - worry about Drake Nevis and Stevan Ridley and Terrance Tolliver (how long has that guy been around?) and mostly about Patrick Peterson, who is the single best player Auburn will see this season. Focus on those things and the rest will take care of itself.

Van: Fair enough. I'll turn off Ebay. For now. But if we beat LSU, I'm going to be back on there, surfing the ticket listings and hotel rooms for Glendale, Arizona again, as frantically as Les Miles trying to get a trick play off with two seconds left and the clock running.

Aaaand see how we did that? Segue to Les Miles! Time to talk the crazy.

If We Lose to This Guy, We'll Never Hear the End of It

We will spare you the usual rehashing of the exceptionally bizarre string of games that makes up the Auburn-LSU rivalry. Blah blah earthquakes, blah blah PAT re-kicks, blah blah missed field goals, etc. Heck, this year Miles by himself has been a one-man oddity. What else is there left to say about him? Somehow he seems the perfect fit for a series that has included "The Interception Game" and "The Barn Burner" and the "Cigar Game." Who better to coach one side in a series defined by its moments of insanity than a coach who is certifiably insane himself?

In point of fact, however, for all its weird incidents and Bermuda Triangle-like moments, this game usually comes down to two very tough, physical teams banging away on one another.   Also, interestingly, in some years when you'd expect a close contest, we've instead seen shocking blowouts, such as 1999, 2002, 2003, and 2009. Is another of these in store on Saturday? Or are we destined to see something along the lines of Les ordering a fake field goal using nine men, from his own two yard line, with one second to go?

With Arkansas, we saw strength against weakness on both sides, and the result was probable carpal tunnel syndrome for the scoreboard operator.   This week, we will see strength against strength (when Auburn has the ball) and weakness against weakness (when LSU has the ball). What does this mean?

Almost certainly it will mean a (much) lower-scoring game. How could it not? In fact, it could look a lot like the Mississippi State game, with points at a premium and more last-second heroics. (Perhaps we'll also learn which is mightier in the fourth quarter: Cam the X-Factor, or the Mad Hatter and his Cosmic Counter-Intuitiveness.)

With strength nullifying strength, we have to look for other advantages to exploit. How about special teams?

Against the Hawgs, Auburn put on their best special teams performance in many years.   Unfortunately, they will have to be really great again on Saturday, because LSU's plan is going to be play good defense, run the ball and steal the game with a few big kick returns from Patrick Peterson. The man is averaging 21 yards per punt return! Against North Carolina he totaled 257 return yards on kicks and punts. To stop him—or at least limit him—Auburn will need the same the kind of excellent gang tackling that we saw last weekend. Contain Peterson and the game is more than half-won.

LSU wants to run the ball, play things close the vest, have their defense shut us down, and then try and steal it in the fourth quarter. In this game last year, the first couple of series on offense were key for Auburn. Bad things happened on that side of the ball and the game spiraled away from us. This Auburn team has done an amazing job of responding to adversity, coming from behind and playing with poise in tough situations.   But I don't think anyone wants to see Auburn in that kind of situation late in the game against LSU—and not just because Miles possesses the freak ability to warp the space-time continuum and the quantum probability fields in the final seconds of a contest. Given LSU's weakness in the passing game, the best thing for Auburn this week is to jump on them with both feet and stay ahead. We need to use *our* offense to keep putting pressure on *their* offense—make them have to take chances. Make them have to do the sorts of things Arkansas felt it had to do late, leading to the Josh Bynes interceptions.

Indeed, the first few series are key again this year, and the questions we'll be looking for answers to during the opening quarter include, "Can Cam successfully run the fabled jet sweep against a defense this fast?" "Can OnnieMac get around the end, or does he lose three yards every time Cam lets him try it?" And "Will LSU's secondary be able to take away the passing option?" The holes our O-Line blasted in the Hawg defense will surely be a lot smaller this week. Our success at imposing our will in the run game on them will dictate most of the rest of the game.

If the (good) Tigers can establish some things against the LSU defense early and move the ball, we should all be feeling good a little over three hours later. If we can do that and also prevent the outcome of the game from coming down to some crazy-@$$ Les Miles decision, we'll feel all the better.

This Week's Wishbone SEC Power Rankings, Eyes-Bugging-Out Edition

We apologize for omitting the Power Rankings last week. The whole "Hex" deal chewed up a lot of space. As you're about to see, things have changed a bit since last we considered this ranking:

The Elite
Auburn. Number four (!!) in the first BCS rankings. What a difference a couple of weeks make, huh? When last we discussed this category, Alabama was the runaway sole occupant. Things, to understate the situation drastically, have changed.

The Very Good
Alabama, Arkansas, LSU, South Carolina, Kentucky. Any of these teams could still end up in the SEC Championship Game (heck, so

could Georgia or Florida). Kentucky makes this category by virtue of beating Carolina and barely losing to Auburn the week before. How on earth did they lose (and so badly!) to Florida? If that game were played this week, the question is not "would Kentucky be favored?" but "by how much?"

The Might Be Good
Georgia. A team with (mostly) good coaches and (mostly) good talent just *had* to turn things around at some point. And they (mostly) seem to have done so. The rest of their games—even a home date with Auburn—don't seem (mostly) impossible. Could the Dawgs have a second-half-of-the-season rally waiting?

The Not Good
Miss State, Florida, Ole Miss, Tennessee. Yes, it does seem bizarre to have a team that's 5-2 and ranked in the Top 25 in this category, while Kentucky is a full two categories higher. But let's face it: beating Florida is no longer the world-shocking accomplishment it was not too long ago. And hanging ten points on them—and failing to complete anything beyond one shovel pass in the entire second half—doesn't make you a "good" team. But the Bulldogs do seem poised to move upward, even as the Gators tumble.

The Wretched
Vanderbilt. This category is also calling out to Tennessee, serenading them ever so softly and gently. The outcome of their almost-overlooked clash with Alabama this weekend will decide if the Dores get some company or not. We're sure they'd appreciate it.

In Other News...

Anyone notice that MSU is now a ranked team? And they're 5-2? And that they beat the Gators in the Swamp? The Wishbone respectfully submitted a few weeks ago that the SC win would look better in the rear view mirror than it did at the time. Now, the MSU game is looking like a bigger win than it did then, too. What's more impressive: Alabama holding Florida to six points in Bryant-Denny, or Miss State holding them to seven points in the Swamp? Mmm hmm.

Speaking of Florida, remember those halcyon days of yesteryear (no, really—last year!) when the Gators were a powerhouse that dominated the mighty SEC East? And it wasn't too long ago that Tennessee and Georgia stood just a hair's breadth below them, ready to pounce into Atlanta at the slightest show of weakness out of Gainesville.

Then came 2010, a year in which the Western Division contenders find themselves hoping that, should they make it to the Championship Game, they get a halfway-decent *South Carolina* squad as their opponent, in order to boost their ranking with the BCS... because (at this point) beating Florida or Georgia would probably do little good at all. And let's not even talk about Tennessee. Ouch.

Twilight Zone stuff, indeed.

With LSU defeated, the sky now truly seemed the limit for this Auburn team. Thoughts of Glendale, Arizona—site of the BCS National Championship Game—danced in the heads of many. For perhaps the first time all season, such thoughts did not feel entirely premature.

In the way stood Ole Miss, coached by the man who had brought misery to several previous high-aiming Tigers squads: Houston Nutt.

But we'd just beaten Arkansas and LSU. Surely, surely, Ole Miss couldn't derail our unstoppable express train now...

– OLE MISS WEEK –

Raising (Our Hopes about Getting to) *Arizona*

The LSU game is behind us now, Tigers fans, and the Ole Miss game lies just ahead. And in the breath-catching space between the two, we find ourselves in somewhat unexpected and relatively uncharted territory—ranked first in the BCS standings. *First*. Not the steady climb to third or even second that most of us probably expected, but freaking *first*. We'd like to savor this feeling. We'd like it to go on forever, of course. But it won't, and we can't. Before us lie two huge traditional contests, a cupcake, and a trap. An honest-to-goodness, get-out-of-Cloud-City-Luke it's a trap! How do we react to this? How do we act? What should we think? Is this a blessing (we're not stuck at #3 this time!) or a curse (good gosh, the bullseye's on us—already!)?

Here now is the Wishbone's meditation in three parts on Auburn's metaphorical yesterday (LSU), today (being ranked first in the BCS), and tomorrow (Ole Miss).

Yesterday: LSU

We won. We won we won we won. (*Massive exhaling of breath*.) Besides the victory, what can we take from it?

We talked last week about in-game tactics like bringing up the safeties and forcing Cam to pass, but in retrospect it's hard to figure how we missed seeing exactly what LSU's overall game plan would be: Limiting the number of times that Auburn's offense had the ball. Cam and company can't score when they're sitting on the bench. For LSU, the best defense was a good offense—and even though they don't claim anything *like* a "good" offense, and indeed don't have the kind of offense (see Arkansas and Kentucky) that does give Auburn trouble, they were able to be effective at executing that strategy for long stretches of the game.

Certainly stellar LSU special teams play went a long way toward furthering that goal. Even when Auburn did manage to hold the Bengal Tigers to short gains, Helton and his punt-team compatriots dropped us time and again up against our own goal line. Some of the blame lands on the shoulders of the usually-reliable Quindarius Carr, who appeared to be assuming the ball would sail over his head and into the end zone. (Gene Chizik, post-game, was quoted as saying, "We can't operate like that. That's a special teams nightmare.") But, again, it's also a credit to LSU's punters for being able to kick the ball in just such a way that it looked that way to Carr but then landed (often with a nice golf-ball-backspin kind of effect) right where they wanted it, and to the other members of their kicking team for quickly surrounding and downing it. Only once do we recall the ball getting past them into the end zone. That's impressive.

By way of comparison, our own special teams play nearly killed us, and in so many ways. Looking back at our ongoing commentary on this site's game day post, we find it riddled with criticisms of that phase of the game—and that only a week after such an exemplary exhibition against Arkansas. The aforementioned punt return misadventures were part of it, sure, but also there was the horrendous offside call on the only kickoff to actually pass through the LSU end zone (that's a penalty that seemingly gets called about once every three years, total), resulting in a surrender of over fifteen free yards to LSU. Our own punting game was vastly underwhelming when compared to theirs. An uncharacteristic missed field goal from relatively close range by Wes Byrum (who, it must be noted, does deserve congratulations for breaking Jon Vaughn's all-time scoring record on Saturday—an accomplishment somewhat overshadowed by the other titanic events of the contest) didn't help matters either. The one thing the special teams did accomplish was to keep Patrick Peterson under relative control on punt returns, and that deserves a nod.

So LSU planned to take advantage of their superiority in special teams, throw in just enough offense to run the clock and keep Cam and company off the field, play their usual strong defense, and generally limit our opportunities for scoring. The upshot of this strategy was that Auburn needed to be productive nearly every time they had the ball. We needed to maximize our opportunities. It brings to mind the 2006 game at South Carolina, where Auburn possessed the ball for the entirety of the third quarter and SC owned it for almost all of the fourth. Talk about needing to take advantage of limited opportunities...!

But one phase of this strategy wasn't really working, and that was obvious almost from the get-go: LSU's mighty defense *couldn't stop us*. We could only stop ourselves.

And that's why we were screaming at the TV and pulling our collective hair out every time Auburn would do something foolish or frustrating to prematurely end a drive. Again, note those words: "*Auburn* would do something." Usually Auburn, not LSU, was mostly responsible for Auburn's drives ending without points. Fannin's fumble... an offensive line penalty here or there... a missed field goal... a too-cute play-call on third and short when all we needed was a yard and everyone in the stadium knew what the safest and most correct call would be—and that LSU couldn't begin to stop it.

We have to pause here to give credit to five great big ol' reasons why that kind of play is unstoppable, and why the running game in general is so overwhelming against all foes right now. Big time SEC games are won at the line of scrimmage and that is where Auburn truly won this game on both sides of the ball. Against most teams, LSU's defense is in the backfield waiting for the running back or standing in the hole waiting to make the tackle. Thanks to an amazing job by the Auburn offensive line the holes were there for Newton, Dyer and McCalebb. You don't rush for that many yards against any defense—much less a great one—unless the offensive line as a unit is taking over the game. And they did. Cam Newton gets (and deserves) lots of adulation, but we need to appreciate the fact that a defense filled with future NFL players was getting pushed all over the field on Saturday afternoon—and there was nothing they could do about it.

Which brings us once again to the 260-pound quarterback in the room. Just as in every game so far this year, when Auburn needed a couple of yards for a first down, there was one tactic that LSU could not stop: letting Cam run straight ahead with the ball. One thing Auburn does, late in games, that has made third and especially fourth quarters so productive for our offense, is to stop being clever and tricky and just let Cam take the game over. Now, there's an argument to be made that it's (partly) the three previous quarters of trickiness that wore the defenses down to such a degree that Cam can just roll over them in the fourth, and that may be true. But, thankfully, when the game has been on the line late and Auburn has absolutely needed to score or to at least maintain control of the ball, either Gus has told Cam to take the ball himself and do his thing, or else Cam has taken the ball in his hands and not let Gus outsmart himself. Either way, it amounts to the same thing: There's no need to be *too* cute when you have a gigantic hammer of a quarterback who can bludgeon the defense into first downs. The Hulk doesn't waste time with elaborate karate or ju jitsu moves. He *smashes*.

Cam smash puny defense. Puny top-ranked defense. Puny *formerly* top-ranked defense. *Raaaarrgghhh!*

On the other side of the ball, Auburn's own much maligned defense held LSU to three first downs—*three first downs!*—in the second half. And that was at a time when LSU consistently had great field position, due to the aforementioned special teams efforts/errors. The defense in blue stepped up on Saturday and made things happen. Sure, they missed some prime chances to do even better. (Where were the safeties on the fleaflicker pass for a touchdown? How did Josh Bynes become the entire defensive backfield on that play?) But Nick Fairley took over that side of the ball and wreaked havoc despite consistent double teams. Jordan Jefferson is going to wake up screaming in bed this week with images of a blue #90 jersey crushing him into the turf. Jeremiah Masoli has to be somewhat nervous; he's seen the last several guys in line ahead of him get eaten up by that big blue monster, and now he knows he's next.

Critiques and criticisms aside, of course, it's important to remember that Auburn *did* win the game, defeating the sixth-ranked team in the country in the process—and no one thinks that was the best we could play. These comments are not intended so much to berate the players for their mistakes in a game where, ultimately, they didn't turn out to matter, but are intended to provide food for thought going *forward*, into the last four games of the year—games that suddenly matter *much, much more* than we ever dreamed they would. And *that* brings us to...

Today: HOLY $#*&!! WE'RE NUMBER 1!

For the first time since 1985, Auburn is ranked #1 in the most important poll. It's hard to believe it's been that long. In the years since then, we've more than flirted with championships, including our awesome 1988 squad that rightly should have played Notre Dame for the title (but that leads us back to LSU, and we're done talking about them now), the 1993-94 "streak" squads that rang up twenty straight while on probation, and the mighty 2004 team that finished undefeated but second in the major polls. None of them ever achieved the lofty ranking of this year's team, this week.

Twenty-five years ago, Bo Jackson led the newly-minted #1 Tigers into Neyland Stadium in Knoxville only to be embarrassed by Tony "Coke is it!" Robinson and the Vols, 38-20. Pat Dye called that game a trap in retrospect, and he was right. The team was not focused and they allowed a future NFL "replacement player" and drug offender to throw for 259 yards and four touchdowns, and to upstage one of the greatest athletes in college football history. Bo was supposed to be featured on the cover of *Sports Illustrated* the next week, but in this case the SI Curse struck early, and Bo's image was replaced by that of Robinson. Our reign at the top was as brief as it was unsatisfying, and it came to an ignominious end. Who would have ever dreamed *a quarter of a century* would go by before we again reached that peak?

Now here we are again, with another mind-bogglingly amazing athlete leading the offense* and another #1 ranking in our pocket. Three weeks in a row a team has been in this spot and gone on the road in a conference game and lost. In the case of Alabama and Oklahoma, going into those games, those two teams felt exactly the way Auburn does right now: "We just beat the toughest team we will face for most of the season on national television and everyone is telling us how great we are." And then they went on the road and things didn't go perfectly, and they found they could not execute like they normally do at home, and the other team was *much* more focused and prepared for the game. And they lost. All of them.

Frighteningly, many Auburn fans are thinking, "Yeah, but that won't happen to us, because we beat LSU and LSU is so much better than Ole Miss." Oh...where to begin? Oklahoma and Alabama were thinking the same thing. Weird stuff happens on the road in conference play. Weird stuff happens when you're ranked #1. Put the two together and you have a nightmare. Houston Nutt knows a win can save his job, so Ole Miss will not hold anything back. Being #1 would be great on January 10, but right now it means a great big target on your back.

Be that as it may, however, Auburn fans have a singular experience that trumps any talk about peaking too soon in the polls and fearing traps and upsets. And we call that experience "2004." That is all that needs to be said. It's hard to imagine any Auburn man or woman would prefer to be further down in the rankings right now, knowing what can happen if you get perpetually stuck behind teams that refuse to lose.

Furthermore, everybody—*everybody*—thinks we're going to lose a game before the end of the season. It's hard to find unanimity among the college football cognoscenti and intelligentsia, but on this point they all concur: Auburn has danced along the edge of destruction too many times already this year to make it through four more games unscathed. They all seem sure it will be Alabama, not Auburn, in the SEC Championship Game and in the BCS Championship. They are, in short, hardly tossing flowers in our path. They're practically hurling down the gauntlet at us, challenging us to even try it. They're all guessing how many weeks it will be before we *inevitably* lose. Nobody believes in us—nobody but ourselves. We're gonna have to scratch and claw every dadgum week to prove them all wrong. That, friends, is a *good* thing. In the immortal words of Carl Spackler, we've got *that* going for us. Which is nice.

So bring on that big, beautiful, frightening, intimidating, *gorgeous* #1, BCS. We will grab it and run with it. And when I say we will run with it, I mean that our 260-pound monster quarterback and his cohorts on the offense will run with it—all the way to the end zone, and to Atlanta, and—if there is any justice in this world—to Glendale, Arizona in January.

Tomorrow: Admiral Ack-Bear and his Rebel Forces

Question: Is the Ole Miss game a trap game of epic proportions? Answer: Does a Rebel Black Bear do his business in the woods? (Actually, we're not really sure *where* he does his business; or, to be honest, what a "Rebel Black Bear" *is*, exactly. Though we think it has something to do with Wookies and the Death Star.)

The fact is that our one game against an offense that matched up well with our defense is over. Now we're back to a team with a good quarterback and nothing much to lose. We foresee lots of uncomfortable moments on Saturday as Ole Miss racks up big yardage throwing the ball. In case you missed it in between weather delays, Ole Miss outgained Arkansas on Saturday—in Fayetteville. Jeremiah Masoli accumulated 425 yards of total offense (327 passing, 98 rushing) and accounted for three touchdowns. So while the Auburn defense was great against LSU, we expect to give up another 375 yards through the air in Oxford. And the Ole Miss offense has allowed the fewest sacks in the SEC with seven in seven games.

The good news for Auburn? Han and Leia and the Ewoks must have succeeded, because that energy shield around Endor (or Oxford) actually *is* down. Ole Miss is last in the SEC in scoring defense, allowing 32 points per game. They are a middle-of-the-pack defense against the run and at the bottom in pass defense and pass efficiency defense. Expect another contest like we saw at Kentucky (ugh!) where Auburn rolls up and down the field for large portions of the game but just can't quite put the other team away.

It comes down to this: If Auburn limits the turnovers, the Tigers will win. Ole Miss isn't going to beat Cam's Army unless said Army helps them do it. Of course, all season long, the team that has proven most dangerous to Auburn is *Auburn*.

Time not to be your own worst enemy, Tigers. Time to put together a complete game, top to bottom. It's the best way to escape the Rebel trap—it's only a trap if you make it one!—and you can also consider it practice for what we'll need to do the final two weeks of the season.

Get those stars and #1 rankings out of your eyes, gentlemen, and focus on the Ack-Bears. You've had plenty of reasons thus far this season to see why it will take a complete effort to win—and plenty of reasons to see why, this year, anything is possible. *Anything*.

This Week's Wishbone SEC Power Rankings, Lofty Heights Edition

The Elite
Auburn. And we're gonna ride this train for as long as it will run.

The Very Good
Alabama, South Carolina, Arkansas, LSU. Alabama seems to be in the process of working out their annual mid-season slump issues and getting back into juggernaut mode—though a good dose of 2010 Tennessee will always help with that. Likewise, this Carolina team appears to be readying itself for its annual late-season swoon—and the Dawgs and Gators say, "Thank you kindly, Gamecocks." LSU has a week to try to get Les Miles's reality-altering flux capacitor working again after Camzilla stomped on it in Doc Brown's lab.

The Might be Good
Mississippi State, Georgia, Kentucky. MSU is on the rise, and no reasonable Auburn fan this season could dare criticize another team for just barely squeaking out a win. Georgia is beginning to look downright scary, which must mean it's almost time for them to play us, as usual. It has to be extremely frustrating to be a Kentucky fan this season, because that squad positively *drips* with promise, and yet they find creative ways to lose, over and over. And now they travel to MSU for a chance to right the ship—or for the Bulldogs to make it six in a row and get up a good head of steam before facing Alabama soon...

The Not Good
Ole Miss, Florida, Tennessee. We really, truly hope the Ack-Bears don't take offense at this ranking and decide to take their vengeance out on Auburn on Saturday. *Focus, men. Focus.*

The Wretched
Vandy. What else is new?

* When Cam runs, psychologically and perceptually, it just doesn't *seem* like Cam is zooming like Bo did-- and then you blink and you realize he's covered 50 yards! And it looks like he's taking each of the defenders for a slow (or not-so-slow) dance along the way, giving each of them in Fred Astaire style a brief moment of attention before moving on. Bo was a missile exploding out of a launch tube and rocketing down the field. Cam is a Brazilian samba dancer working his dance card in fifty-yard sessions and ten-yard strides.

** The other side of the BCS ranking issue is that, after 2004, we just despise the BCS. We would hate to see Missouri and/or Michigan State to go undefeated and achieve their best season in fifty years and then have to watch someone else—even Auburn!— play in the BCS title game. (We wouldn't hate it enough to want them to go *instead* of Auburn, of course! But the system still sucks, and we all know it.) There should be a playoff. Even a plus-one is better than what we have now. Whether Auburn is #1 or not, the system still sucks, and Auburn taking advantage of it for a change, rather than being the victim of it, won't change that fact.

In retrospect, we didn't learn a whole lot from the Ole Miss game that we didn't already know. We got behind early and came roaring back—and we already knew we could do that. We knew defenses could stop Cam for brief stretches but not for an entire game, and we saw this happen once again. And we knew Houston Nutt would come up with a challenging game plan—and he probably did, but Cam and Co. still managed to make him look silly.

Perhaps the most famous thing to come from this game, looking back on it now, is the one new thing we learned: Cam can catch, too! He lined up for one play at receiver, and good ol' Kodi Burns chucked him the ball, and he dominated the Rebel DB in the air and came down with a touchdown reception.

The relief of getting a win over Ole Miss and closing out that super-tough mid-season portion of the schedule lasted only a couple of days, however. Just long enough, as it turned out, for John and Van to write the next week's column. A day or so after they turned it in, the first reports surfaced claiming that Cam Newton had solicited payments to sign with Mississippi State.

What followed was a week of abject misery, as Tigers fans wrung their hands and pored over every word coming to us via the mainstream media and the blogosphere. By the time of kickoff for the Chattanooga game, the Auburn Family was in desperate need of being able to focus solely on football, rather than on rumor and innuendo. There has probably never been a game in AU history of such little immediate football consequence, and yet of such dramatic psychological consequence. Football as psychotherapy...

– CHATTANOOGA WEEK –

10

More Bullets in Our Gun

As the Auburn football team relaxes a bit (for the first time in a long time!) before gearing up for the annual Amen Corner finish (still huge but much diminished from some of those epic 1980s Amen Corners that included Florida and FSU in addition to UGA and Alabama—sheesh!), the Wishbone also takes the opportunity to dial it down a notch or two. This week we survey the overall state of affairs with regard to the Loveliest Village—where we stand, what's to come, and what people (and our machine overlords) are saying about us. We do so using the ever-popular "bullet point" model. And speaking of "bullets"...

* More bullets in our gun.

Over and over this season we've heard the refrain: "Auburn is a one-man team." And then came the Ole Miss game.

No one seems entirely certain whether Dr. Gustav and company went to Oxford with the *plan* to sort of replicate what we did against Louisiana-Monroe a few weeks ago—intentionally hold Cam in the pocket and have him just dish and deal the rock to his increasingly-impressive supporting cast—or whether it came as a result of what Nix and the Ole Miss defense were doing, or some combination thereof. In any case, it turned out not to matter, because that supporting cast more than stepped up and showed its abilities and its potential for the rest of the way.

Defensive coordinators across the land had to be wetting their pants at such a display. After all, the talk throughout the week building up to kickoff was, "How do you stop Cam Newton from running all over your defense?" Paul Finebaum must have asked some variation of that question to every single person he interviewed, chatted with, or bought a cheeseburger from last week alone. Sure enough, the Rebels (maybe) found an answer—and all they got for their troubles was another Auburn 500-yard performance, the fresh and now-healthy legs of Mike Dyer unleashed, and 51 points hung on their scoreboard.

A one-man team? Georgia and Alabama only *wish* we were. Come to think of it, so do the last nine teams we've played.

* More bullets waiting for Alabama.

Malzhan revealed a few more cards from his hand at Oxford—and in the process he gave defensive coordinators *even more* to think about. We know from last year that he probably has five or six extra-special plays he's keeping under wraps, specifically for Alabama. We speculate that they are currently locked inside a triple-reinforced, lead-lined, adamantium/vibranium alloy box, designed to protect the mere mortals inside the football complex from the massive gamma radiation emitted by their sheer brilliance. It goes without saying that we're very much looking forward to seeing them in action.

Of course, in our heart of hearts, we hope that such plays aren't even needed. What more glorious vision could a true Auburn person conjure up in his or her imagination than the sight of Cam and Dyer and Onnie Mac simply slicing and dicing and slashing their way through the heart of the Tide defense, straight-up, with no trickery whatsoever? What wouldn't we give to see Cam truck a Bama linebacker into the end zone? Furthermore, what impression would such a display make on the poll voters? And since we're mentioning the BCS...

* The three favorite topics during the BCS show.

During Sunday's BCS rankings show—which, incidentally, proves that ESPN can make a big, dramatic production out of *anything*—three main topics consumed most of the airtime: 1. Oregon sure is great! And, as a corollary to that, Auburn needs to be winning with "style points." 2. Alabama is a real threat to get into the National Championship Game! 3. Cam Newton is <u>NOT</u> a lock for the Heisman!

Topic 1 is understandable. Oregon's offense is remarkable (though we have to think that at least some Duck fans are saying the same thing about Auburn's) and more than deserves all the attention it's getting. And they did jump Auburn for first in the BCS rankings. To say Auburn should be winning with more "style points," however, strikes us as absurd. The Tigers have rung up multiple games of 500+ yards of total offense, including shattering LSU's all-time ground-conceding record. They've pasted 65 on Arkansas and 51 on Ole Miss—you know, two teams from the SEC West, called by many the toughest single conference/division in all of college football. This past weekend, they unleashed a rookie running back for nearly 200 yards, tore off a long kickoff return for a touchdown, and even demonstrated Cam Newton's (remarkable) pass-catching skills as he scored a touchdown in yet another manner—as a receiver. Tell us that Tommy Tuberville's 2006 squad needed more offensive flair and we'll wholeheartedly agree. Tell us that *this* Auburn team lacks style and we will call you a raving lunatic.

The third topic—the trophy isn't Cam's quite yet!—reflects ESPN's desire to provoke and promote argument with regard to the Heisman for the simple reason that it's rarely been this much of a runaway so early in the season, and they get a lot more talk-show mileage out of a big debate than out of a done-deal. It's simply no fun for their shows or for their commentators if they are forced to admit that the race is already over. Honestly, that's probably a good thing for Cam, or at least for Auburn, too. It keeps the subject of the Heisman (and Cam) on people's lips a bit more than if it were considered a total fait accompli and the subject were ignored the rest of the way.

Now let's look at that second topic. My goodness, but you could hardly turn on sports-talk TV or radio over the past couple of weeks without hearing umpteen scenarios for how and why Alabama could and should make the BCS Title Game. The intricate justifications which are always included involve the SEC's strength as a conference, Alabama's loss occurring early enough in the season for the Tide to have "time to recover in the polls," the semi-"perfect storm" Alabama walked into in Columbia, and their fearsome reputation as defending national champions with last year's Heisman winner.

Taken as implicit in every one of the scenarios, however, is Alabama defeating three foes with a combined record (as of this week) of 23-3! That includes, of course, beating undefeated Auburn on the day after Thanksgiving—and, indeed, the perception here is that most of the national sports media members seem to strongly *favor* Alabama in that contest.

They are of course welcome to favor whomever they wish for that game. This can, however, be turned to Auburn's advantage. Even when Auburn was (briefly) ranked first in the BCS last week, and as many talking heads fretted over whether the young men who make up the team could stand up to that kind of pressure, the prognosticators were still largely talking about ways in which the *Tide* could and would make it to the SEC Championship and the BCS game. In other words—just because you're ranked first or second, Auburn, doesn't mean the human voters have confidence that you will go all the way, guys. You're still the hunter, not the hunted. You are still the team with something to prove to the country. There is and should not be any complacency on the Plains. Motivation aplenty is available. Just listen to the commentators still dreaming of finding a way to put Alabama into the big post-season games instead of you, and get all fired up about that, and then take those feelings out on the Dawgs and Tide.

* Why Auburn dropping to #2 in the BCS is a *good* thing.

Speaking of motivational tools, the Tigers have to be somewhat miffed that their stay atop the BCS lasted only a week. Dropping to second isn't disastrous in "2004" terms, obviously, but it's still kind of annoying, especially since they didn't, y'know, *lose a game* or anything. Let's be honest, though. We were all somewhat taken aback by the Great Leap Forward to first last week, and the thought of wearing the biggest bullseye the rest of the way wasn't terribly appealing. Here, then, are three ways in which Auburn dropping to second in the BCS rankings is actually a good thing:

1. The aforementioned bullseye now hovers over Eugene, Oregon, instead of Auburn, Alabama. We would much prefer to play in a potential national title game as the hunter than the hunted. The only downside is that the Tigers would be wearing their all-whites instead of the best uniforms in college football. And the Ducks would be wearing one of their 8,000 eye-gouging combinations that look like the Jamaican flag melted over a steel girder.

2. Motivation for our team. You've been dissed by the BCS, guys! If you make it to the end and get to play in Glendale, take out that resentment and anger on the opposition!

3. In the event that Alabama should win the Iron Bowl, they'll want to receive as much benefit from such a victory as possible in order to jump over the undefeated but non-AQ teams ahead of them. Beating the #2 team isn't quite as impressive as beating #1. We will admit, though, that this "benefit" is somewhat akin to hoping the shark that eats you later develops severe heartburn.

* Defense Wins Championships. Right?

We've all heard that old saying for most of our football-watching lives. But, for the first time, we're starting to question just how true it is, or at least if there can ever be exceptions to it.

The idea is that defense is more important in the long run to a championship-seeking team because strong defense always shows up, while in some games a good offense has a bad day or is stymied by a smart defensive game plan.

Here's the problem with that, at least with regard to this year's Auburn team: This year, ever since it found its stride after Clemson, our offense always shows up. It shows up, and it erases mistakes— mistakes by the defense, the special teams, and even by itself.

In the Ole Miss game, the Rebel Bear Calamari creatures employed a completely different offensive approach (according to Ted Roof) than they had used previously this season. It didn't much work. Even if it had, though, their offense would have had to score at least 52 points to win. They'd probably have had to score even more, in fact, because our offense wouldn't have spent much of the fourth quarter slowing the game down and running the clock—they'd have approached the situation more like they did against Arkansas, just keeping the pedal to the medal and racking up an inconceivably insurmountable lead.

Maybe in a different year—even last year with that great Alabama defense—there would be more cause for concern. But this year we simply don't see a dominant defense on the scene that appears capable of totally shutting the Auburn offense down. Or, to be fair, Oregon's offense, either.

This year—if the situation holds, and maybe for this year only—*offense wins championships.* Speaking of which:

* There's a column to be written about a hypothetical Auburn-Oregon matchup, with all the fireworks that such a thing would imply.

And if fate smiles upon us in a way it hasn't upon Auburn in decades, we'll be able to write that column soon.

* We're beginning to think Alabama fans would trade losses to LSU and Miss State for a win over Auburn.

Don't believe us? Just listen to the Finebaum program for any thirty-minute stretch this week. Then again, why subject yourself to that? Just believe us.

Best evidence we've heard thus far? A Bama fan caller on Tuesday was pleading with/demanding from Brother Oliver some sort of reassurance that Coaches Richt and Saban must, even now, surely be dreaming up monstrous and heretofore unheard-of defensive schemes to utterly shut down that fraud Cam Newton. The tone of the caller's voice was such that any reasonable listener could imagine the man feverishly wringing his hands while gazing imploringly up at his black velvet portrait of the Bear. Oliver's response? "They've got their hands full." Surely not what the Alabama Nation wanted to hear—not from their patron saint of shutting down scary offenses. Finebaum cut off any comeback with one of his more reasonable and level-headed observations ever: "That game is not for three more weeks."

The problem is, we're not entirely sure Alabama Fan understands that.

* The party of the elephant is, paradoxically, great for the Tigers.

Finally, in this election week, a teaser for a longer article to come from the Wishbone in 2011: Auburn football always does better in years when the Republican Party is rising or in ascendance. Alabama, conversely, has enjoyed its brightest football days when the Democratic Party was dominant.

We of the Wishbone make no representation here about our own political views, or about the parties or candidates themselves. That entire side of the matter is wholly irrelevant to our purposes here. We merely present the (quite bizarre and inexplicable) fact that having the party of the elephants and the color red in ascendance tends to (paradoxically) result in Auburn doing much better on the football field than the Tigers do in the years of Democratic dominance. From Shug's greatest teams during the Eisenhower years, to Alabama's titles in the 1960s and 70s under Kennedy, Johnson, and Carter, to Pat Dye's glory years coinciding with Reagan's, to Alabama's last two national titles coming during the first years of Presidents Clinton and Obama... it's strange, yes, but very true.

So as we watch the outcome of this year's elections rolling in, and as we see the big Republican wave of victory across the US, we of the Wishbone have to admit a *completely non-political* happiness about it. This could be just the omen we need to guarantee a crystal football coming to the Plains in a few months.

Or it all could be complete garbage. Who's to say? We'll find out in January...!

The Wishbone Mailbag

This week's Mailbag brings us the following query:

-- Why didn't Cam Newton make the tackle on that long run by Ole Miss at the start of the game? Doesn't he possess the Power Cosmic, allowing him to alter reality such that he can suddenly appear among the defensive backfield? --P. Dye, Macon Co., AL

While it is true that Cam does possess the Power Cosmic, likely from a heretofore undocumented encounter with Galactus, we have ascertained that, during that play, he was busy rescuing the entire population of a town in Albania after its local dam broke, as well as pulling Timmy from the well. Sometimes even touchdown-saving tackles must take a backseat to the lives of thousands of Albanians (and Timmy), whether we like it or not.

The Wishbone Power Rankings

The Elite:
Auburn

The Very Good:
Alabama, Arkansas, LSU, Miss State, South Carolina. Alabama edges slightly ahead of this pack, though it's a real jumble at this point. The LSU-Bama game on Saturday will tell us a lot. Miss State has become a real threat to beat Alabama—who saw that coming in August, or even in September? Bama's schedule suddenly looks tougher than ours—they play at LSU on Saturday, then home against Mullin's Dawgs, and then (after the Curry Bowl) the Iron Bowl. Miss State could move past Arkansas and even LSU in the bowl order for SEC teams before all is said and done. Wow.

The Might be Good:
Florida, Georgia, Kentucky. Florida edges ahead of UGA by edging past them at the Cocktail Party (and don't you imagine there was a good bit of drinking going on after that game, by both fan bases—but for entirely opposite reasons?). Poor Kentucky—we can't shake the feeling that they're a good team; with just a little more defense they could be a serious contender, at least in the SEC East.

The Not Good:
Ole Miss. Getting torched by the Auburn offense will make anyone look bad, though. As with Kentucky, you have to feel there's some potential here, but...

The Wretched:

Vanderbilt, Tennessee. Welcome to the bottom, Vols. Yes, it has come to this. But just remember: You have that famously lightweight UT November schedule with which to try to salvage...well, something.

Georgia Week.

As the showdown with Auburn's oldest and (perhaps) most respected foes drew near, talk still swirled nonstop about Cam and the allegations against him.

Actually getting to play a game (Chattanooga) had proven remarkably therapeutic, moving the attention of the fans and players and media away from all the "smoke" for at least a few hours. Remarkably, Cam's performance sparkled; one scarcely would have guessed that he was the center of the biggest controversy in all of sports at that moment.

With that game behind us, we all looked ahead to Georgia and we understood that somehow the players and coaches were going to have to refocus themselves on the business at hand. Otherwise, a season that had come (almost from nowhere) to hold such remarkable promise could dissolve into dissention and defeat.

It is a tribute to the togetherness and the mental fortitude and the resilience of the players and coaches of this Auburn team that they put all those distractions aside and took care of business on the field—and against such a historically dangerous opponent.

Just how *historically dangerous, the Wishbone devoted an entire column to explaining...*

11

Auburn-Georgia: The Past is Prologue

Van leads off this installment of the Wishbone with his personal recollections on the Auburn-Georgia series. John chimes in here and there with some notes of his own. In the next installment, coming in a day or two, they'll break down the strategic and tactical dimensions of this year's contest.

I have always considered the "modern era" of Auburn football to have begun in 1982, and I chose that year for at least three important reasons: 1) It was Pat Dye's second year, but the first in which he had a really good team with a winning record and a bowl win; 2) it was Bo Jackson's freshman year, and in my view the advent of Bo marks the beginning of modern Auburn football; and 3) it was the first year I really paid close attention to the team, following the games on television (or more often via Jim Fyffe's radio broadcasts).
So here, then, I present a look back at the more consequential and eventful games in the Deep South's Oldest Rivalry—from a more personal perspective.

The **1982** game will always be the answer to a great trivia question: Did Bo Jackson and Herschel Walker ever face one another in a game? Indeed they did. We don't have the exact yardage totals handy, but you can get the gist of this clash by NetFlixing the *Incredible Hulk* movie and just fast-forwarding to the Green Goliath's big throw-down with the Abomination. The Tigers played a monster of a game—and were throwing into the Dawgs' end zone on the final play for the win—but Georgia held the Tigers off and eked out a narrow victory on the Plains.

Then Walker turned pro, and Bo went on to dominate the extremely hard-nosed **1983** matchup in Athens. This 13-7 victory ended Georgia's run of SEC titles as the Tigers ultimately seized the "team of the decade" designation away from Athens and to Auburn in the eyes of many. It was also the first time I ever saw the opposing team's cheerleaders crying their eyes out on television.

Two years later, in **1985**, Bo bravely battled his way through the Georgia game on national television—with not a few Heisman voters watching. Late in the game, the announcers revealed that he was playing with broken ribs. The previous year, Jerry Gray of Texas had nearly ripped Bo's arm off at the shoulder, and Bo had basically told the trainers, "Staple the &#% thing back on—or not; I'll play without it!" So a few broken ribs were no problem for the mighty Bo. He ran for a ton of yards and Auburn won; a few weeks later, he had his Heisman. This was the game that put him over the top, just as it had Pat Sullivan, fourteen years earlier.

Can we safely assume that all good Auburn fans (and Georgia fans) know the story of **1986**? Auburn was playing for a share of the SEC title and possibly a Sugar Bowl berth; their only loss had been a miracle comeback by the Gators in Gainesville a couple of weeks earlier. Georgia was playing without their starting quarterback. So of course the Dawgs led the game late. A furious effort by Brent Fullwood on the ground and Burger-to-Tillman through the air (in what was probably Lawyer's breakout game) could have won it, but Fullwood's late touchdown run was called back on a phantom penalty. The Dawgs got the win, stormed the field, began ripping up sections of the turf, and refused to leave; so the AU officials turned the stadium's water cannons on the fans on the field and still in the stands. Georgia's howls of protest didn't die down for months, but Auburn made the best of it, with Aubie showing up the next year brandishing a garden hose with a pistol-sprayer, and T-shirts everywhere bearing the catchphrase the game will always be remembered for: "Nothing Stinks Like a Wet Dawg."

John chimes in with his memories of the 1987 game:

The **1987** clash in Sanford Stadium, the year following the "hosing" incident, was a great game. Auburn fans showed up in Athens wearing ponchos and rain gear, and UGA fans responded by shooting us with water guns. Georgia was ranked eighth going into the game and Auburn was ranked twelfth. The defense performed well, Lawyer Tillman made a big play and Auburn pulled out the win. Important lesson learned from this game: When Auburn is ahead in Athens, get down early to rip off a big piece of the hedge to bring home. Later in the game they station quite a few police around the hedges. (I got my piece but others waited too long and were denied.) The other best moment from this visit? After spending the evening at several favorite watering holes, we staggered back across the UGA campus. I noticed a large bell on a tower with a rope hanging down. A UGA student told me, "It is rung after victories." In my 3 a.m., out-partying-all-night state, it made perfect sense to me to go running across the lawn, grab the rope and yank on it with all my weight, ringing that bell as loud as I could, disturbing everyone on campus. It made sense at the time – because Auburn had won!

Now back to Van:

Even Pat Dye said the **1989** team didn't really come together for most of the season (maybe he lost his pants a few times along the way, throwing off the game plans)—until they pulled off a dominating 20-3 win in Athens. That's pretty late in the season to be finally coming together... unless the game after it is the "*First Time Ever*" with Alabama in Jordan-Hare, also known as the single most important Iron Bowl ever.

The only memorable things about the **1990** game, aside from being another Auburn win in the series, was that I was a senior and I believed it was my last time as a student to see the Tigers play in Jordan-Hare (laughable in hindsight, given my years of graduate school to come), and sending Vince Dooley into coaching retirement with a loss to his alma mater. John and I had staked out the best seats in the student section all season long for our little crowd of friends, and this game was a great capper for us, rounding out a season that had also included a huge come-from-behind draw with Johnny Majors' Tennessee and a spectacular last-second win over Florida State.

John and I watched the **1992** game on television in his apartment in northern Virginia—we were both in graduate school at Georgetown that year. We watched Auburn drive down the field in the final seconds, trailing by four, only to have time expire as the Tigers attempted to get off one last play from the UGA goal line after a bobbled handoff prevented a touchdown on the previous play. Ray Goff was signaling frantically for his defensive players to lie down on the ball and not let the referees reset it, and for some unknown reason the zebras never bothered to stop the clock for that purpose. The Dawgs never would have stopped James Bostic on the dive, but it was not to be. We watched helplessly and dejectedly, a thousand miles away, as this all transpired; then we spent the evening drinking beer and cursing the refs.

By the time of the **1993** game, I was back in Auburn and the Tigers were rolling along at a shocking 9-0 in Terry Bowden's first season. We'd beaten Florida earlier in the year and the team just had an aura about it; somehow we all just *knew* we were going to find a way to win out. So confident was I, I had about a dozen blue t-shirts printed up before we traveled to Athens for the game that read, "10 and 0 and One to Go!" When Auburn went up 42-28 late in the fourth, my friends and I in the upper deck of Sanford Stadium busted the bag open and spread 'em around, to the annoyance of the Dawgs fans all around us. Part of the shouting match that ensued included a UGA fan noting that Auburn was not going to a bowl game. One of my friends reminded him in turn that while UGA was, unlike probation-shackled but undefeated Auburn, legally *eligible*, the Dawgs weren't going to a bowl game simply because their team *sucked*.

In the **1994** game in Jordan-Hare, the Bulldogs accomplished what two bouts with Spurrier's Gators had been unable to do; what an LSU team with a big fourth-quarter lead had been unable to do; what Alabama had been unable to do. They ended Terry Bowden's magical twenty-game winning streak. Matt Hawkins missed a field goal at the end that would have won it. Noted philosopher Ray Goff commented afterward, "You don't just *win* all the time." Certainly you would know, Ray. Meanwhile, I knew immediately that I shouldn't have had a "Red Dog" beer at Niffer's before the game.

The **1995** Auburn-Georgia game in Athens was the coldest football game I've ever attended, or at least it felt that way to me. I blame the weatherman. The forecast called for moderate temperatures and rain, so I dressed in a very thin jacket and short sleeve shirt. As it turned out, never a drop of rain fell, but the thermometer plunged. Toward the end, as Auburn was hanging on for the victory, Georgia fans began to rip out whole sections of the fabled Sanford hedges—which was actually okay with the authorities, because the field had to be widened ahead of the next summer's Olympic soccer matches, and they were planning to rip out the hedges anyway and replant new ones the next year. I was so cold by then, if I'd had a match I'd have set that celebrated shrubbery on fire. Oh, and then we couldn't find our car after the game, so we wandered around the darkened Athens campus, totally lost, for something like an hour as the temperature dropped lower and lower. But it was okay; I didn't mind it all that much. Somehow, winning makes that kind of stuff a lot more bearable.

The **1996** game was in the bag—a victory!—with UGA out of timeouts and the clock trickling away. And then an Auburn player touched the ball, causing the ref to blow the clock dead and reposition it. In the time that it took to do this, Georgia's offense lined up again and got off one last play—a touchdown pass that triggered the first overtime in SEC history. The game had taken at turn for the weird earlier on, when Uga *the Overrated Mascot* nearly spayed and/or neutered Auburn WR Robert Baker *the Coke Deal Maker* as he ran out of bounds. (Who knew Uga had been given DEA training?) Several OT sessions later, with both teams scoring almost at will, the situation had grown nearly unbearable. It was a night ESPN game to begin with, meaning late start and longer than average commercial breaks; but once you added in all that overtime plus the time change at the Georgia border, we were looking at getting back to Gwinnett County at about four in the morning. I actually looked to my companion and said, "At this point, I almost don't care if we win or lose—I just want this over!" A few plays later, when the Dawg defense stopped Dameyune Craig on fourth down, I had my wish. Unfortunately. Me and my big mouth.

95

Aside from an Auburn victory and 45 points courtesy of Craig and company, the most memorable thing about the **1997** game for me was the method by which I gained entry to Sanford Stadium. Now, listen—I'm not entirely proud of this today. But you have to understand, it was Auburn-Georgia and so I did what I had to do. I had for some reason waited until almost the last minute to decide to go to the game, keeping my streak of attending AU-UGA games in Athens alive for another cycle, but I was alone and didn't have a ticket. So I put on my Georgetown University windbreaker (with its bulldog logo—you see where this is going, right?) over my Auburn jersey and zipped it up tight to my neck, hiding my AU cap under it. Then I scalped a ticket from a friendly Dawg fan outside the stadium right before kickoff.

The poor guy. I wasn't very subtle or tactful. As soon as the money and ticket changed hands, I unzipped my jacket to reveal the jersey and put on my hat. He rolled his eyes and visibly sunk inward, perhaps comprehending the great disservice he had just performed for Bulldog Nation. Indeed, for the next three-plus hours, I gave that particular red-clad section of Sanford Stadium my best. Probably three hundred faithful Dawg fans were looking daggers at me the entire time. Thank goodness (and Craig to Karsten Bailey) we won, or I might not have made it out of there alive.

In **1999** a pretty mediocre Auburn team that ended the season at 5-6 rolled into Athens and absolutely *shellacked* a Georgia squad that was headed toward an 8-4 record and an Outback Bowl win. The Tigers, with virtually no running game, somehow led 31-0 at halftime and then scored on their opening possession of the second half to go up 38-0, at which point Georgia fans were streaming for the exits. This was possibly the greatest game for Auburn WR Ronney Daniels, who (on the receiving end of Ben Leard's passes) simply could not be stopped by the Bulldog defense.

I attended the game with a good friend who graduated from Georgia, and he paid me beforehand for tickets for him and his AU-fan girlfriend. I bought the tickets weeks before the game, and then discovered on game day that I had somehow misplaced them. (Three years later, while moving to a new apartment, I actually found the three original tickets in a little envelope in my desk drawer—right where I had put them in 1999.)

So I had to hurry from Lawrenceville to Athens in order to get there in time to find some replacements. In my haste, I made a wrong turn—hard to do when you realize Highway 316 runs directly from Lawrenceville to Athens!—and didn't realize it until I neared the outskirts of Conyers. If you know anything about Georgia geography, you'll know this is not good, particularly when time is of the essence. I finally reached the UGA campus shortly before game time, frantically located my friend, found more tickets, and got into the stadium just in time for kickoff.

During the game, and particularly early on, as the Tigers were absolutely dominating the Dawgs and simply rolling up and down the field, my friend had to endure constant high fives being exchanged over his head by me and his girlfriend. I've always felt bad about that, because he was so classy about it. But this was such a shocking win, so out-of-the-blue against a good Georgia team, that even now I can't quite believe how we blew them out. It was just one of those nights. As with the 1995 game, sometimes a win on the field makes everything else not nearly as bad or as important.

The **2000** game was the Rudi Johnson game, and also served to break the long streak of the visiting team winning. It took overtime, but on this OT occasion the Tigers prevailed, pushing the Tigers one step closer to their second SEC Championship Game appearance. Unfortunately for me, this game also marked the breaking of my own streak of attendance—it was the first time I missed seeing an AU-UGA game in person since 1992—because I'd promised to attend a friend's music recital. No, I can't quite believe it, either. I didn't even get to watch the game live; I recorded it on a VCR and desperately avoided hearing anything about it until I could get home and watch. Rudi's game-winning touchdown came (for me) at around 2 a.m., reminding me of the end of the other OT game in 1996—except that it seemed like that game actually *did* end around 2 a.m.

If 2000 was the Rudi Johnson Show, **2001** was the Cadillac Williams Extravaganza. Coach Tuberville and the offensive staff had been leaning on Caddy more and more during the season, mostly because neither Jason Campbell nor Daniel Cobb could quite get the passing game working. By the Georgia game, Caddy *was* the offense, getting something like forty carries in the win. This was the game where, afterward, Tubby admonished SEC rookie coach Mark Richt that he'd never win in this conference without running the ball a lot. Caddy could definitely attest that night that Tubby had no problem doing so.

I think of the **2002** game and I still get a little sick at my stomach, for several reasons. Auburn was having an up-and-down season, losing to Ron Zook's Florida when we should have won but somehow absolutely demolishing Nick Saban's LSU. This was the year of Bobby Petrino as Offensive Coordinator and the Cobb/Campbell monster throwing to a bevy of freshman receivers. It was also the year that Caddy broke his leg against the Gators and we all discovered that *Ronnie Brown Lives*!

Georgia that year was arguably one of the best SEC teams of the decade. Their only loss was an inexplicable egg they laid against Florida; otherwise this pack of Dawgs would have been in the running for the national championship. Despite their quality, though, the Tigers had them on the ropes late. One more first down run from Ronnie Brown and the game would have been over. But Ronnie had gotten hurt a little earlier—he would miss the Iron Bowl, opening the door for the celebrated Tre Smith Miracle—and try as he might, he couldn't convert. Georgia got the ball back, and a short time later we all got to experience the misery called "70-X Takeoff," a play that resulted in Michael Johnson outleaping Horace Willis for the game-winner.

This particular play has gone down in Southeastern Conference history, though few people seem to realize it. As far as I can tell, it was the first time (and perhaps the *only* time) that a single play in a single game changed *both* participants in the SEC Championship Game. If Willis had knocked that ball down, Auburn would have won the SEC West, and would have faced the Florida Gators in the Georgia Dome. Instead, the Dawgs claimed the East title and faced Arkansas. Crazy. (A Gator friend actually emailed me after that game, complaining about our failure to defeat Georgia and thus put Florida into the title game. He railed that the Gators would have made short work of Arkansas. He backed off quickly when I pointed out that Florida would have faced *Auburn* instead of the Hawgs.)

The next morning I found that my car had been broken into and my stereo stolen. The humiliation was complete. I sold the car a couple of weeks later, and I can't say it wasn't entirely because the memories associated with it had simply become too tainted. When I looked at that old Honda, all I saw was, "70-X Takeoff." It had to go. Think of it as an exorcism.

I don't recall the **2003** game fondly, either. It was the culmination of a bitterly disappointing season in which we started the year riding high, amid national proclamations that we might win the national championship. Of course we ended up farther from even an appearance in the SEC Title Game than in any other year of our great 2000-2007 run. Auburn was absolutely inept in this game, the Dawg fans in Sanford Stadium were merciless, and I left at halftime. That was the first time I'd ever left an Auburn game before the end. I was there by myself, amid a swarm of irate Auburn students who alternated between criticizing the team and yelling insults at the Georgia students nearby, and I simply couldn't stand it anymore. Horrible, horrible.

The opposite side of that coin, of course, was the **2004** game in Jordan-Hare. Most anyone reading these words understands the significance of that game. Georgia was a top ten team, their only loss coming (somewhat surprisingly) to eventual East champs Tennessee earlier in the year. We needed to beat them and beat them thoroughly in order to gain whatever advantage might be gained over #1 USC or #2 Oklahoma, who were both stubbornly refusing to lose.

Beat them thoroughly we did. Some have called this the single greatest performance by an Auburn team in the modern era, and that may well be true. Cadillac Williams even passed for a touchdown in this game, and Georgia would have been shut out but for a controversial score just before the end. I still remember my dad being absolutely furious that Georgia had scored. I tried to point out to him that we were now 10-0 and that we'd totally crushed them in a way we rarely had in my memory. He didn't care. "I wanted to shut them out!" he barked—and he was right. Bless that man's heart, for it is in the right place.

I ended up watching the **2005** game on television in a sports bar in Lawrenceville, the only Auburn fan adrift in a sea of red and black. I'd just gotten back from a couple of months living in Singapore (long story) and was out of work and broke, so I didn't feel right about driving down 316 and trying to find a ticket with money I didn't have. Oh, if only I'd thrown caution to the wind! Fourth down… Cox to Aromashodu… Fumble…   Recovery… Clock runs down… Field goal… WIN!

And that, my friends, believe it or not, was the *last time* we beat Georgia.

The **2006** game was a disaster, of course. My wife and I had just started dating a short time earlier and this was the first Auburn game she ever watched. She did not see me at my best that day. To my embarrassment, my confident pronouncements to her about my Tigers' national title aspirations utterly evaporated in the wake of Matthew Stafford's carpet bombing of the Auburn secondary. As for the three games since then— **2007-2009** —together they constitute one continuous and awful blur for me. All I remember from any of them is Auburn doing fairly well at first, only to see Georgia roaring back and finishing the Tigers off late.

John adds a word of warning here:

Going back over these games, it seems that this series, more than any other Auburn plays, is one where the lower ranking team *can win* the game.   A quick review of the games since 1982 reveals upsets in 1983, 1986, 1987, 1994, 1996, 1999, 2006, and possibly in other years. That should serve as a warning to this Auburn team— do not take Georgia lightly because of their record, or the fact that they lost to the worst team in the Big 12. Stay focused. This is *Georgia*.

Van wraps things up:

The Oldest Rivalry in the Deep South, indeed—and one filled with history, for the teams and the players and the universities, but also for each fan who has been a part of it along the way, each Auburn Man or Woman who lent his or her voice to the din of the crowd; who helped to collectively will the team to victory in a given year. This is a series filled with upsets and championship denials on both sides; derailings aplenty. This is a series that flashes a blinding "Warning! Warning!" in letters twenty miles high to any team for which hubris has become a possibility. Championships that one or the other team has just begun to reach out to embrace have a way of evaporating to nothingness for the favored team under the harsh lights of Sanford Stadium or Jordan-Hare.

Enough of that! For the Auburn-Georgia series—a series all about history—the past is prologue. It's time to reverse the recent curse. It's time for Auburn to reclaim the upper hand in this rivalry, which as of now stands with the Tigers holding a microscopically slender one-game lead after more than a century of epic battles. It's time for Auburn to beat the Dawgs with a rolled-up newspaper— preferably a newspaper filled with exciting photos of Cam Newton running roughshod over the rest of the SEC competition. It's time to take care of business against Georgia—business long deferred and now more than overdue.

Plain and simple: It's time to *Beat Georgia*.

In the 1990s, Georgia put their coaches' pictures on the tickets. Little-known fact: Uga and a cheerleader actually co-coached the team in 1997.

So with the Auburn-Georgia history lesson completed, the Wishbone went from looking back to looking forward, and turned our attention to the game at hand.

The first installment was called "The Past is Prologue" because the two programs had clinched championships—or spoiled them for the other side—so many times in the past, and because the unique flavor of the Auburn-Georgia rivalry is so tied to history—not just sporting history, but also sociological, economic, geographic, and political history.

The second half of the Georgia preview was called "Prologue to a Championship" because a win by Auburn would give the Tigers the SEC West title and book their tickets to Atlanta—and do so a game before the Iron Bowl, a contest which (in terms of winning the SEC, at least) would be rendered meaningless. Given the predictions of Alabama perhaps repeating as national or at least SEC champions, this was something that had been utterly unthinkable at the start of the season. Even those optimistic souls who believed Auburn had any chance of winning the SEC in 2010 had surely believed the road to Atlanta ran through Tuscaloosa. For the Tigers to wrap up the division with a game to spare—well, the sheer improbability of it all demonstrated just how "dreamlike" this season was becoming.

The task ahead was not an easy one, however. While the Bulldogs had struggled early in the year, they now had their prolific receiver, A. J. Green, back from suspension and were hitting on all cylinders. No one expected the much-maligned Auburn pass defense to completely shut down Green and his compatriots on the Georgia side, but we hoped that some way, somehow, the Dawgs could be limited enough for the Auburn offense to outscore them...

– GEORGIA WEEK , Part Two–

12

Auburn-Georgia: Prologue to a Championship

Enough with the Georgia nay-saying, people!

Everywhere we've turned in the last couple of days, on those rare occasions when we've been able to find honest-to-goodness Auburn vs. Georgia *football* talk (as opposed to talk about you-know-what), all we've been seeing is warning after warning, admonition after admonition about how Georgia is in such a prime position to knock Auburn off and spoil the drive to Atlanta (and maybe beyond).

If you read our previous column, you know (if you didn't already) that Georgia and Auburn have a long and storied history of spoiling one another's good seasons—when the team that loses really had something to play for on the line. Those who are trying to find a scenario whereby that could happen again this year have been working some of the following angles:

1. Georgia's offense has started clicking in recent weeks and they could light up our famously accommodating defense. Their defense is playing better, too.

It's true that Georgia (5-5 overall, 3-4 in the SEC) has scored thirty or more points in five straight games. So we can reasonably expect them to top that number again Saturday. But—if you haven't been watching closely, you might have missed it—Auburn's defense has been getting better over the past few weeks. Roof has been dialing up more blitzes and has changed up the coverages in the secondary more that he was before, and these adjustments were somewhat effective against Ole Miss. It doesn't hurt that we get back a few defensive players from injury, too—or at least have more of them available if needed. The Tigers are still running mostly a "bend but don't break" sort of scheme but, given the improvement, there's a chance Auburn may surprise us all with a strong showing on defense.

But let's be honest. Georgia is a much more dangerous offensive team than Ole Miss was. Forget the games they lost early in the season when A.J. Green was out; Uga has his groove back now. The offense is comparable statistically to South Carolina and the defense is comparable to Arkansas. (It could be worse: they could be Arkansas on offense—yikes!—and South Carolina on... um... never mind.) Their big weakness on defense has been on third down, where Georgia is eleventh in the SEC in allowing opponents to convert on third down (over 40% of the time). Meanwhile, Auburn has been one of the best third down teams in the nation this season on offense. So that does not bode well for the Dawgs.

At quarterback, Aaron Murray is having a nice season (60% completion rate, fifteen touchdowns, six interceptions). He looks like the real deal, and should only improve as he gains more experience with the offense. It doesn't hurt that he has a great target to throw to in the aforementioned A. J. Green, either. They have achieved something approaching balance on offense thanks to the running of sophomore Washaun Ealey. He's looked serviceable if not spectacular through ten games this season.

Based on what we've seen from Auburn's defense this season, we have to believe that the Bulldogs are going to make a lot of plays on Saturday. As with the Arkansas game, it's probably just going to happen. Defensive coaches have obliquely referenced this in some of their comments to the media this week, stressing that our defensive backs have to be able to put bad plays behind them, recover mentally and focus on the next play, and "not get beaten twice by the same mistake."

On defense, in the first year of new defensive coordinator Todd Grantham, Georgia plays a 3-4, something Auburn has not seen this season. There will probably be some plays early in the game where the difference in assignments causes problems for the Auburn offense. This will be a big test for the offensive line, backs and receivers in picking the right person to block.

Justin Houston is an excellent outside linebacker for a 3-4 defense and the NFL scouts love him. He has passed Nick Fairley for the lead in sacks in the SEC so he will be a big test for the Auburn tackles and running backs when he comes after Cam. At 6' 3" and 258 pounds, he will provide a heavyweight matchup when he rushes Cam or when Cam runs to Houston's side.

Georgia is starting a talented true freshman at strong safety, Alex Ogletree. He has a lot of potential, but being a safety facing the misdirection and ball fakes of the Auburn offense could cause him a few problems, so look for Auburn to take advantage there.

Georgia's special teams have been very good this year. Both their kickers have played to All-SEC levels (Blair Walsh is 17 of 20 on field goals), and their kick-coverage units have done excellent jobs. No wonder the Tiger coaches this week were so unhappy with Quindarius Carr dropping a punt and our punting duo doing such a mediocre job; I mean, they would have been upset anyway, but in a week where we're facing one of the best special teams units we've seen all year, our problems in that area recently are particularly troubling.

2. The visiting team does well in this series, as does the underdog.

Historically the "visiting team" thing is true, and the 1990s were the epitome of this phenomenon, with Auburn winning in Athens in 1993, 1995, 1997, and 1999, while Georgia won in Auburn in 1992, 1994 (well, it was a tie but might as well have been a loss for us), 1996, and 1998.

The two programs have also derailed one another from championship runs on multiple occasions, the most recent and vivid of which for Auburn would probably be 1986, 2002, and 2006. We can remember doing it to them a couple of times in the 1970s and especially 1983, too.

In the grand scheme of the series, though, such happenings are relatively rare, and there are plenty of other things that should occupy our collective minds before this. It's hard to see how something that happened in 1978 could have much impact on whether the Dawgs can stop Cam on Saturday, or on if the Auburn secondary can limit A. J. Green. Speaking of whom:

3. Georgia is a different team on offense now that A. J. Green is back.

The more we study the individual tactical matchups and the overall strategic milieu of this game, the more we feel that it all comes down to this: "Stop A. J. Green." We talked in our column earlier this week about the astounding day Auburn receiver Ronney Daniels had against UGA in 1999. If Green can put together something approaching that kind of dominating performance, Georgia can win. At the very least, a transcendent Green could cause this game to closely resemble the Kentucky contest in October, if not the Arkansas track meet, where Auburn had no choice but to keep scoring and win a shootout. If, on the other hand, Green can be held to something like four catches for fifty yards, then everything else becomes much more difficult for Georgia and we should reasonably be able to predict that the Tigers will crush them.

4. Auburn lost to Georgia for the last four years, so maybe they have our number, like Florida has theirs.

Ridiculous. Auburn's endured several negative runs of late, including three wins in a row by LSU and a couple by Arkansas. Those curses didn't seem to matter much this season. Georgia is more than overdue to have their string against us snapped. They've eked out narrow escapes in most of those wins, or at least the Tigers kept things close until late in the game. They've lived on borrowed time against Auburn for too long now, and the only number of ours Georgia will be seeing a lot of will be a white "2" on a blue background, coming right at them, over and over.

5. Georgia has nothing to lose and can play with reckless abandon, while the Tigers (with more on the line) could come out tight.

This Auburn team hasn't shown the slightest inclination toward getting "tight" as the season has worn on and the stakes have gotten higher. To the contrary—as the challenges have become stiffer, the Tigers have grown stronger. The improvement of the offensive line, the blocking by the receivers, the running of Mike Dyer—all of these things point toward little possibility of a letdown on Saturday, or the rest of the season.

As for Georgia, while they have improved their fortunes of late, they have yet to beat a team with a winning record. How will *they* respond if Auburn's offense starts moving the ball consistently and grabs an early lead? In the four SEC games the Dawgs have lost thus far this season, they never led. If they fall behind again, how will they respond—reckless abandon or not?

6. Georgia is trying desperately to qualify for a bowl game, so they're really hungry and will bring greater-than-expected effort.

Sure, Georgia wants to get to a bowl game. But does anyone truly believe that the Dawgs' desire to make it to Shreveport or Memphis is somehow greater than the Tigers' hunger to clinch the freakin' SEC Western Division title, secure a spot in the SEC Championship Game in Atlanta, and keep alive the hope of making it to Glendale, Arizona for the National Championship Game? *Seriously*?

7. Auburn will be distracted by you-know-what.

Up through Tuesday of this week, we felt like that was unlikely. The players were saying all the right things—things along the lines of, *If it doesn't bother Cam, it doesn't bother us*—and the coaches were fiercely defending our quarterback. The situation had taken something of a downward turn by Wednesday, though, with talk of admissions and FBI intervention and whatnot. We can't know how these developments will change the situation until we see it with our own eyes.

What doesn't kill you makes you stronger, they say. If that's true, the Tigers should be breathing fire at 2:30 on Saturday.

So, in sum, take your nay-saying and your curses and your away-field-advantages and *stick* them. This game will be decided between two teams on the field, one of which has a ton of things to play for, and is well aware of that fact—but is not overwhelmed by it.

If all goes as it should, Saturday's game should turn out to be another glorious triumph for the Tigers in this storied series—and also something more: *A prologue to a championship.* (Or two.)

John's Not Looking Ahead, buuuut....

C'mon, y'all—it's the Iron Bowl. And John has a few thoughts about it. Here we go:

You thought the fun was over after Les Miles chewed up the Tide along with the Tiger Stadium turf last weekend? Nope. Miss State's defense is going to give Alabama a hard time on Saturday night. They will be able to shut down the run. The Tide will win at the end but the home fans in Tuscaloosa will be unhappy leaving the stadium—imagine that—because they will know what is coming next.

Alabama's 2010 football team that won the big crystal football is clearly not as good as the 2009 edition—but sometimes you need numbers to confirm what your eyes are telling you. The two key areas are pass rush and protecting the passer.

The table below shows the 2009 Alabama stats (through the same number of weeks) and then the 2010 stats. In these three categories Alabama is significantly worse than last season. (By contrast, Ole Miss, which did a great job of containing Mr. Fairley and company, is now number one in the SEC in fewest sacks allowed at less than one per game.)

Alabama 2009
Sacks: national rank 14, 2.88 average, SEC rank 1
Tackles for loss: national rank 18, 7.38 average, SEC rank 1
Sacks allowed: national rank 12, 1 average, SEC rank 1

Alabama 2010
Sacks: national rank 105, 4.22 average, SEC rank 12
Tackles for loss: national rank 95, 4.78 average, SEC rank 12
Sacks allowed: national rank 100, 2.78 average, SEC rank 10

What do these things mean for Auburn?

Alabama is not nearly as good as LSU or South Carolina on the defensive line and not as good as Ole Miss or South Carolina on the offensive line. Against our offensive line, Alabama is going to have a hard time improving these numbers. Look at that again: the Alabama defense, home of all five-star recruits, is *last* in sacks and tackles for losses in the SEC.

And while Alabama is more balanced offensively this season, they are allowing a lot more sacks on the pass attempts they do make. After watching Drake Nevis dominate them last week, Alabama has to be genuinely afraid of Nick Fairley and what he will do their offense.

The Wishbone Mailbag

Dear Wishbone,
I have heard that it is wise for Georgia fans to pack a poncho or other water-resistant clothing before venturing to the Plains, as occasional rainstorms can sweep through Jordan-Hare Stadium. Please advise.
H. Dawg, Athens, GA

Dear H. Dawg,
While it is true that, at least in one past Auburn-Georgia contest, a rainstorm did unexpectedly materialize at the end of the game, we must point out that this was a highly unusual occurrence. The rainstorm in question struck at the end of the game for only a short time and was extremely localized; it covered only the visitors' sections and part of the playing field. Almost magically, it ended once the Georgia fans departed the stadium. Consequently, we do not see a tremendous likelihood of such an event happening again—*unless certain Dawgs didn't get the message last time.*

The Wishbone's SEC Power Rankings,
Afraid-to-Turn-on-the-TV Edition

The Elite: Auburn.
That is, as long as certain *off*-the-field talk doesn't start affecting *on*-the-field play.

The Very Good: LSU, Alabama, Arkansas, Miss State, Florida.
There's been a lot of movement in the middle of the pack all season, and it continues this week. LSU has proven you can be very good without (at times) much of an offense, and Auburn has proven you can be elite without (at times) very much of a defense. Alabama's estimation in the eyes of the pundits certainly has taken a beating in the days since they were licked by that cud-chewing lunatic in Baton Rouge, while MSU's has risen steadily (as long as we're talking about performance on the field and not rumor mongering). So the Tide-Dawg showdown on Saturday should be most interesting to watch. Arkansas opened up a serious can of hot sauce on Carolina last weekend and pounded the poultry flat enough to make chicken parmesan. And who knows what to make of Florida? We can only hope to find out in Atlanta in a few weeks...

The Might Be Good: South Carolina, Georgia, Kentucky.
They should have removed the calendars from the locker room at Williams-Bryce. Apparently the Gamecocks saw that we'd reached the outskirts of November and decided to perform their annual swoon. Georgia we'll know a bit more about in a couple of days. Kentucky has a chance to make a bowl game and finish the year on a high note, but if only they could have played with a bit more consistency this year they would have had a season to remember.

The Not Good: Nobody this week.
Quite a drop-off down to:

The Wretched: Tennessee, Vanderbilt.
And neither seems ready to move up any time soon, though we suppose one of them has to actually win their season-ending showdown in a couple of weeks.

*In the end, the Georgia game will probably be remembered mostly for the controversy surrounding Nick Fairley's...shall we say...*extremely enthusiastic *pursuit and tackling of Dawgs QB Aaron Murray. Talk about his hits—late or otherwise—swirled for days after the game, dominating the blogosphere and souring the usually decent relations between the two fan bases.*

That's unfortunate. Arguments aside about just how egregious Fairley's actions were, this was a very entertaining game that saw both teams play well, particularly on offense, and a lot of points fly up on the scoreboard. It deserves to be remembered for what was accomplished on the field by two teams playing at a high level.

Once again, the Tigers allowed an opposing receiver to rack up major yardage—a trend that would, sadly, continue with the Alabama game. Carolina, Arkansas, Georgia, and Alabama all had receivers post almost two hundred yard games against the Auburn defense. It's a testament to just how resilient and determined to win this Tigers squad was, that they found ways to overcome that major shortcoming.

With the Georgia game in the books, Auburn looked ahead to a long-awaited open week before time to face Alabama in Tuscaloosa. But did the Wishbone columnists join their Tigers in taking the week off? To the contrary! Instead, they cranked out two *columns prior to Bama Week...*

What, Chicken Again?!

It's an off-week, so Van and John roll out a potpourri of observations and arguments, looking back at the Georgia game and forward to the next two big ones, to tide us over for a couple of days.

Auburn-Related Stuff on Van's Mind this Week

* Victory over Georgia.

Sweet indeed. Living in Atlanta from 1995 to 2006, I came to appreciate the glorious feeling that comes with knocking off to the Dawgs. Previously, having grown up in Alabama, the Georgia game never meant all that much to me. Eleven years in Georgia and I totally got it. When you hear Auburn players who grew up in Georgia say how much it means to them to beat the Dawgs—*believe it.*

* What, chicken again?!

Playing Florida in Atlanta would have been satisfying in so many ways. There's the history angle: In our second appearance in the Dome in 2000 we faced the Gators, and it wasn't close or pretty. Just as we got the chance to even the scales with Tennessee in 2004, paying them back for 1997 (I still cringe, thinking about Manning-to-Price late in the fourth), it would have been fantastic to get the chance to balance the books with Florida. There's also all the stuff floating around lately about Urban Meyer's possible role in the Newton imbroglio. Finally, there's the prestige (and the pure fun) of smacking down Florida, and possibly ringing them up for a third loss to us in a row. Indeed, it would have been joyous.

Alas, instead we get a heaping helping of reheated chicken on the artificial turf. A team we've already taken down once. It's almost always tougher to beat a team a second time in the same season, as Tennessee demonstrated in 2004 by giving us something of a struggle in the Dome, after we'd absolutely taken the lumber to them in their own house earlier that fall. So it's sort of disappointing to miss out on a shot at the Gators—and if you *ever* wanted to play them, this is the year.

At least we get the satisfaction of facing our old and respected foe, Steve Spurrier, one more time. Every time we hang an "L" in his ledger, it makes up (somewhat) for that abominable run we had against his Gators between 1995 and 2000. No, it's never a disappointment to have to face Steve Spurrier. And I have no doubt we will have our work more than cut out for us in the Georgia Dome on December 4.

And let's face it—a win over *anybody* from the East, if it comes in the Dome and they're the other division's representative in the Championship Game, means an SEC Title for us. And that's all that really matters.

* Zeitgeist at the Belleville Burger King in Southern Illinois on Monday, when Van walked in wearing an Auburn jacket:
Overwhelmingly pro-Cam, completely unsolicited. They love him.

*Cam has now become the first SEC player to pass for more than 2000 yards and run for more than 1000
But, honestly, doesn't it feel more like the other way around?

* "On behalf of."
Perhaps the key phrase in whatever legal wrangling will eventually settle the Newton controversy. As Bill Clinton might say, it depends on what your definition of "behalf" is. Some might argue that for one person to act on "behalf" of another, there would have to be a knowing connection—that you're doing something for someone

because they *asked* you to, or at least that you are *aware* of it. If Cam wasn't aware of and didn't request for Cecil to ask for anything, was Cecil really acting "on behalf of" Cam? Especially if Cam was a grown man by that point, and not a child, whose parents sort of automatically act on kids' behalf? This could be the sticking point upon which any eventual NCAA ruling hinges.

* Man, Eric Smith blocks so well.
On the next to last touchdown in the Georgia game—the second pass to Lutzenkirchen—Smith blew up the UGA defensive end so Cam could have time to throw the ball. It was so well-designed, too: the whole play flowed to the right, and Smith even started out in the fullback/h-back spot on the right side of the formation. But when the ball was snapped, he ran left (even as nearly every other Auburn player was moving right) and completely walled-off the DE. Beautiful.

* It's okay, Coach Grantham.
Nobody else has been able to figure out how to stop us, either.

* Water cannons in Jordan-Hare:
Good for 'em in 1986; probably wouldn't have hurt this time, either.

* Sour grapes:
The only thing from Athens that stinks worse than a wet Dawg.

* Georgia whining:
Keeping that happy post-victory buzz going for another 24 hours.

* Former Georgia quarterback Buck Belue says:
"Fairley would be a rock star in Georgia if he played for the 'Dogs. But he plays for Auburn. So we hate him. I get it." 'Nuff said.

* Les Miles is already lobbying to get LSU into the BCS Title Game.
No, I'm not kidding. He's making that argument. But—just imagine if Oregon and TCU and Boise State all lost before the end of the season. You say it would defy the laws of physics and of nature? *Exactly.* This is Les Miles we're talking about.

* South Carolina did look awfully scary on Saturday in the Swamp—

—scary enough to make everyone apparently forget how Auburn handled them, when our offense wasn't as proficient as it is now; and perhaps more significantly, just how thoroughly Arkansas blew them out only a little over a week ago. Our degree of concern should be at a healthy but not irrational level, heading to Atlanta.

* Anyone else see Oregon trying to play more like Auburn on Saturday?

Their final drive, keeping the ball out of Cal's hands for something like nine minutes, was strangely reminiscent of our last drive against Kentucky. Oregon likes to brag that they play super-fast, all the time, but now we know that they can also slow it down and grind it out—if it's that or lose.

* Poll voters who voted Oregon #1 ahead of Auburn on Sunday

were in effect saying that they didn't think Auburn could have scored fifteen points against Cal. It's bad enough for the Ducks to be ranked ahead of us with such a weak schedule compared to ours but, after the Cal game, it's become downright insulting. (Not to mention insulting to our intelligence.)

* Nausea-inducement quotient, sliding scale:

A couple of Long Island Teas and a ride on a Tilt-a-Whirl < raw pork chop served in a dirty ashtray < whining Georgia fans.

* But! Whining Georgia fans being the (seemingly endless) story...

= Less talk about *Cam Cam Cam*. At least for the first part of this week.

* Except for!

Finebaum. Dredging up old Cam stuff from Friday, all day long on Monday. And then wall-to-wall Fairley, all day on Tuesday. What did we expect?

* Then there's Gary Danielson,

who actually covered the game live for CBS, and then re-watched it on television afterward—and pretty much sided with Fairley on every point other than the flagged late hit (which no rational Auburn person has defended). His only critique was to suggest Chizik should have called a timeout to remind his players that they shouldn't do anything of a retaliatory nature that might endanger their playing status for the next opponent, since it's Alabama. Wow—what a stinging indictment of Auburn's behavior. I can't imagine how Georgia fans must have reacted.

* And also Spenser Tillman,
   who agreed on Wednesday morning that Fairley is not a "dirty player," echoing Danielson almost exactly. Almost made me want to take back the Barry Switzer/cocaine/machine guns in the dorm insults I was hurling at my TV on Saturday during the studio segments.

*And let's also not forget that Chop Block U.—
   —is now no longer us!

And Now—Several Points *John* Wishes to Make This Week:

* A few words about Mr. Nick Fairley.
   He is *not* a dirty football player. He has made some plays this year that should have been (or were) penalized. He has made plays that, in the "quarterback is a porcelain doll" world of the NFL, would have gotten him fined. (But college football is different—the NFL has gone too far in protecting the quarterback so when people watch a college game they expect to see the same restraint.)
   In the Georgia game Fairley made several plays that angered the UGA team. In the first quarter with the score 14-7 and UGA near midfield, he hit Aaron Murray straight on and drove him into the turf. (Several times this year Fairley has picked up the opposing quarterback and spiked them into the ground, landing on top of them.) Again, this is a penalty in the NFL but not in college. Go change the rules if you don't like it.
   I love Nick Fairley and I hope he wins the Outland and Lombardi trophies *but* we all know he took some cheap shots at Murray he did not need to. And that is what helped cause the riot at the end. However, the other part of it, that UGA will never admit, is that Richt came in and told his team "You can't back down—you have to

hit them in the mouth and get inside their head" and they did that to us in the first quarter. But after we settled down and played our game, that didn't work anymore—it only contributed to the growing bad feelings [*which the refs didn't do much to control, either—Van*]. There's also the fact that all these guys know each other and the Auburn guys who are from the state of Georgia were tired of losing to UGA, and their frustrations showed.

The worst part is that all of that silliness above causes Goggans and Blanc to miss the first half of the Alabama game. And we freaking need them. I guarantee this: Chizik ripped the team into little pieces on Sunday. He was not happy.

In his defense, Fairley was both chop-blocked and held regularly in the game. Not that either did UGA any good in stopping him. The one play I thought was the most egregious (sorry - for the bama fans reading this, that means "over the line") was the hit near the goal line when Fairley speared Murray in the back after the ball was thrown. This should have been a penalty; the officials missed it and this contributed to the frustration of the Georgia players.

At the end of the game, UGA had the ball near midfield with 2:03 left in the game, down 18 points. Mark Richt could have called a running play and gotten on the bus and gone home. Instead he called a fifty-yard pass that required his talented young quarterback to take a seven step drop and hold the ball, against a defensive line they'd had problems blocking all day. The game was *over*—UGA's chances of coming back and winning at that point were about one in a billion. Are those odds worth risking the best young quarterback in the SEC over? *No* – but Richt did it anyway. To me, there is no difference between this play and the Tyrone Prothro play: in both cases the game was over but the head coach refused to acknowledge it and someone got hurt because of that.

But do you know what else Nick Fairley is? He is *intimidating*. SEC quarterbacks are afraid when they play Auburn. Their eye level drops from looking down the field to trying to find Fairley. They worry about where he is and what he's doing and this impacts their play. So do you know who is whining and crying even more than the typical Georgia fan this week about Fairley? The typical Alabama fan. After watching Drake Nevis puree the center of their offensive line they are scared of seeing Nick Fairley making regular and unwelcome visits to their backfield on Friday afternoon.

And here is the real danger for Auburn fans. All this whining—all this crying about dirty play—is serving to push the refs into looking much more carefully at Fairley, and being potentially much more likely to flag him for more penalties. Others (particularly Tony Barnhart) have noted that exact factor this week, particularly after the SEC reviewed the game tapes and opted not to further penalize Fairley. But the very fact that they felt it necessary to announce that he *wasn't* being penalized shows just how closely they're looking at him.

Nick Fairley is a defensive lineman. His job is to get into the backfield and tackle the ball carrier. If his target is the quarterback, he wants to hit the guy so hard that he is intimidated and will be more likely to throw the ball away later on. If Fairley commits a penalty in the process of his work, the refs should call it. Otherwise, the whining fans should shut up and sit back and prepare to watch him crush the Bama quarterbacks, like he has done to everyone else this year.

* Auburn's players lost their composure twice on Saturday—

at the beginning and at the end. If they do that in any of the next three games, we lose. It cannot happen again.

* Bama is the most complete team we will play all season.

They are very good at everything—not *great* at any one thing but, unlike other teams we have played, they don't have a single real weakness. We will just have to go in there and outscore them. Did you see Saban chewing out the backup quarterback when they were up 30-3? He knows what is coming on November 26 and he knows that his team will have to play great to win. And the crowd in Bryant-Denny will be insane from the pre-game on. This is Auburn's toughest game of the year and no mistake.

* Cam showed something on Saturday in the passing game.

The throw he zipped down the middle to the *Swede Killa* for a touchdown was an NFL throw. He made two or three other throws that must have had NFL scouts saying *"Yes!"* That was the best he has thrown the ball all year, even with the two huge drops in the first half.

* Aaron Murray is a very good player

and he is going to torment us the next three years. He's the best young quarterback in the conference.

* If we can stop the run we can beat Bama.

That is the key. Last year we stopped the run but could not score enough. This year we can score plenty. So Bama will try a ball control approach and keep it away from us, limiting the number of possessions in the game, the way LSU did. We have to get it back in the hands of our offense.

* I love how Malzahn puts a few more cards on the table every game.

Against Georgia it was the unbalanced line thing (complete with hurry-up to the snap, to disguise it). And it was really nice. So now Alabama has to prepare for that as well as everything else...*except* that you just know Malzahn has five or six *more* cards up his sleeve just for that game.

*Beat bama!!!!!!!!!!!

This next one is pretty much self-explanatory. With the regular season nearing its conclusion and the biggest game of any year looming just ahead, the Wishbone engaged in a little wistful contemplation of what we had all just witnessed over the previous few months...

Evolution of a Dream

With our team resting and recuperating and preparing for that biggest game of any season—the Iron Bowl, of course—the Wishbone takes this opportunity to look back at the eleven games that have preceded it.

We asked ourselves, "What did we think about our team and the season and each particular game during the week *before* it was played, and then how did we see those same things the week *after*?" We wanted to take a look at just how our hopes and dreams and (even the occasional) rational expectations have changed as our Tigers have progressed—quite literally *progressed*—through the season.

Additionally, we tossed in our week-by-week feelings about the Alabama game, because they are Alabama and we are Auburn and thus, whether we like it or not, we think about them 365 days a year, more or less.

So, without further ado, here are the eleven games of the 2010 Auburn Tigers football season to date, along with the zeitgeist surrounding each of them:

Game 1: September 4: **Arkansas State**, 52-26
Before: "I just want to beat Georgia this year. And go to a decent bowl game. That would indicate significant progress, I think." And also, "Can't wait to see this new quarterback and running back in action. From all the YouTube clips and recruiting stories, they both should be really fun to watch." And finally, "Well, Phil Steele says we could be 11-0 when we go to Tuscaloosa. Sounds crazy to me, but he's uncannily accurate most times, so...we'll see."
After: "Offense looks really good. Newton could be even better than advertised. Everyone's criticizing the defense, and especially the secondary. We gave up 26 to these guys. Ouch. I suppose 9-4 would be the best we can hope for—but that's improvement."
Regarding Bama: "They're monstrous. We're going to get killed, just like we've figured all off-season."

Game 2: September 9: at **Mississippi State**, 17-14
Before: "This will be a tough road game. Mullen has them improving. We need to win this one because there are several others down the way a bit that should be a lot harder."
After: "Whew! A narrow escape! But hey—any road win in the SEC is a good win."
Regarding Bama: "They're monstrous. We're going to get killed, just like we've figured all off-season."

Game 3: September 18: **Clemson**, 27-24 (OT)
Before: "This will be a tough one. Again, though, there will be tougher tests ahead, so if we're going to even match last year's win total—with this game in the place of West Virginia—we need to find a way. And, hey, this Clemson team has numerous Bama ties, so there's at least a bit of motivation to whip 'em!"
After: "What a come-from-behind win! This team is at least resilient. That Clemson quarterback is a tough kid, and Clemson's going to win some games this year. Good gosh, we really have to do something about the short pass defense! And even the offensive line isn't playing the way we hoped."
Regarding Bama: "They're monstrous. We're going to get killed, just like we've figured all off-season."

September 25: **South Carolina**, 35-27

Before: "This is the best team we've played thus far. Lattimore is looking like a better get for them than Dyer was for us. Can we stop him *and* stop Garcia and Spurrier's passing game? We've been very fortunate so far this year, but I don't like our chances very much in this one."

After: "What a win! Cam really looks like something else! The offensive line played better, the defense shut down Lattimore entirely, and we held their offense late in the game when we had to—including causing four consecutive turnovers at the end. And there went Spurrier being Spurrier again, benching his senior QB in the fourth quarter. Thanks, Steve!" And, "That was a pivotal win, in terms of how the season ultimately comes out. We'll have to blow a game or two against easier competition to have things go terribly wrong now."

Regarding Bama: "Maybe there's a slight chance? Well, probably not, but more than we might have thought previously."

October 2: **Louisiana-Monroe**, 52-3

Before: "Tune-up before we get back into conference play."

After: "Nice plan of Malzahn's to have Cam almost entirely throw the ball. He looks pretty darned good doing that."

Regarding Bama: "They just destroyed Florida and now look like they could give the lower half of the NFL a decent game. Maybe Cam gives us a slightly better chance that we expected, but honestly I don't see anyone beating them this year."

October 9: at **Kentucky**, 37-34

Before: "They beat us last year, in Auburn. They have several extremely talented players on offense. I'm very nervous. But aren't their fans here outside the stadium (and then inside) so nice!" [This was the one game this year I was able to attend in person.]

After: "We won we won we won! But good grief, we could not stop their passing game! Clearly we have severe problems against offenses that feature quarterbacks getting rid of the ball quickly, particularly on screens. And our tackling has not been great all season."

Regarding Bama: "OH MY GOODNESS. SOUTH CAROLINA!!"

October 16: **Arkansas**, 65-43
Before: "This will be our toughest test of the year. They do everything on offense well that we don't defend well. Mallet's playing very well. Their defense is better than last year—and they beat us last year. How on Earth will we be able to hang with them? Let's face it—this is the one we finally lose."
After: "Are you kidding me? SIXTY-FIVE?! Now I'm starting to believe that we can play with anyone, because no matter how much the other team scores, we can somehow score more. Maybe this really is the year that *offense* wins a championship."
Regarding Bama: "Well, well, well. They're mortal after all. Who knew? Maybe, just maybe, we have a shot in that game."

October 23: **LSU**, 24-17
Before: "This is the first game all season, against a seriously tough foe, that I've actually felt an above-average level of comfort. Part of it is that we're doing so much better than I expected; part of it is that we just hung sixty-freakin'-five on Arkansas; and part of it is that this game is sort of the polar opposite of the Arkansas game— we have a weak defense but they have a weak offense, and vice versa. Maybe I'm being overconfident, but I like our chances."
After: "DID YOU SEE THAT RUN BY CAM?!"
Regarding Bama: "If we can beat LSU that way, we certainly can compete with Bama. Starting to believe...!"

October 30: at **Mississippi**, 51-31
Before: "It's a road game in the SEC, and we are as of now the #1 team in the BCS. Everyone says we are primed for a letdown, and this could be the perfect 'trap' game. And of course Houston Nutt has had a way of messing with us through the years."
After: "Cam can even *catch* touchdowns! Not #1 anymore? Actually, maybe that's a good thing—as long as we don't drop below second. Moving on..."
Regarding Bama: Comfort level actually increasing. We are the #2 team in the BCS and they have two losses. If that game was in Jordan-Hare, I would feel totally confident. But now *we* are the team with a destiny, and *they* could be the spoiler, the biggest hurdle in our path. Amazing how the Fates have changed jerseys, huh?"

November 6: **Chattanooga**, 62-24
Before: "CECIL DID WHAT?!?!"
After: "Okay, that was sort of a nice palate-cleanser. Now—back to,   CECIL   DID   WHAT?!"
Regarding Bama: "Another loss? To Les Miles, noted cud-chewing lunatic? How the mighty have fallen. I am starting to feel exceptionally good about the Alabama game... provided nothing else bad comes along, news-wise..."

November 13: **Georgia**, 49-31
Before: "We just need to play some football, and get this week of horrifying news behind us—at least for an afternoon. Georgia's beaten us four years in a row. That's unacceptable and has to stop now. Will Cam play? Can the rest of the team focus on the game, despite all the distractions? *Will Cam play??*"
After: "Not pretty at first, but not the first time we've had to do that this year. VICTORY. This team does not get flustered even down double-digits. They know how to respond. Cam played and DID he ever play. Fairley... so much to praise, so much to wince about. Even so, this Georgia complaining—this *fixation*—on and about him is just pitiful. They're mad about losing, about Richt, and about having 49 hung on them and they're focusing all their frustrations on Fairley. Whatever. Nothing stinks like a whiny Dawg. Still very disappointing to be down two defensive linemen for the entire first half against Alabama. Do the Georgia fans intend to keep whining all the way into next season?"
Regarding Bama: "Thirteen days to rest and get ready..."

November 26: **Alabama**, ??-??
Before: "What will Malzahn dream up between now and then? What can Roof and Chizik come up with to at least limit Julio Jones? Can they shut down the two backs the way they did last year? What new bombshells will detonate in the media? How many days can Finebaum make the Cam story and the Fairley (non-)story drag on? How will Saban try to manipulate the refs into calling stuff on Fairley if he even breathes hard on McElroy? How will the team respond, playing in that stadium in that environment?"

The Wishbone Mailbag

Dear Wishbone:
I represent certain business interests in the nation of Nigeria. For an investment of only $180,000, you will receive many millions of dollars later. Of course, you can't let anyone know you have invested this money, as that could blow up the entire deal. Well, I say it would blow up the deal, but really it would only blow you up. We'll still get our millions. Interested?
—K. R., Starkville, MS

Dear K.R.,
And here we'd thought you left town with Jackie Sherrill.
—The Wishbone

The Wishbone's SEC Power Rankings, Off-Week Abbreviated Edition

The Elite: Auburn.
Our various foes and critics think we're being obstinate in plodding ahead with the season in the face of nearly daily allegations against everyone not named Cam Newton himself or Auburn University. We see it differently—we think all of those details were conveyed to Auburn and to the SEC weeks ago (mostly by Cam's dad) and all we're seeing now is a steady drip drip drip of details (some possibly accurate, some probably not) emerging to the public that Auburn already knows about and has already factored into its decisions. That's not obstinacy, it's being ahead of the story.

The Very Good: LSU, Alabama, Arkansas, South Carolina.
We're promoting SC into this category if only because they hammered Florida in the Swamp and qualified for Atlanta.

The Might Be Good: Miss State, Florida, Georgia, Kentucky.
You can't take beatings like (three of) these guys did and not drop a bit.

The Not Good: Tennessee.

Do a number like that on Ole Miss and you at least get to move back up out of the "Wretched" category.

The Wretched: Ole Miss, Vanderbilt.
You enjoyed a few weeks off the bottom of the barrel, rebels, but come on—you can't go out and embarrass yourselves the way you did in Knoxville and not drop back down, if only for this week.

And then, after an interminable wait and yet somehow all of a sudden, Bama Week was upon us.

The SEC Western Division title had already been decided—Auburn had it in their back pocket. The tickets to Atlanta had been booked. The Georgia Dome awaited. In the grand scheme of things, the Iron Bowl mattered only in terms of Auburn's overall and conference records, and the Tigers' position in the national championship race.

Of course, in the state of Alabama, it mattered much, much more than that. In the state of Alabama, winning the Iron Bowl is everything. And the Tigers would be going in to face the defending national champions in their newly-expanded house, beneath the gaze of more than a hundred thousand rabid Tide fans.

The possibility of letdown was very real. The challenge was immense. How the game played out would tell us so very much about this Auburn team's abilities and about their mind set.

Indeed it did.

What we witnessed next was something that will be remembered and discussed for as long as they play football in the state of Alabama...

– ALABAMA WEEK –

The Hate that keeps us Warm

The Colonel: "All that hate's gonna burn you up, kid."
Robert: "It keeps me warm. "
--from "Red Dawn"

So here we go. The big one. The Iron Bowl.

It's for pride. It's for bragging rights. It's for an undefeated regular season. It's the last step on the journey to Atlanta. It's a step closer to Cam's Heisman, and a step closer to Glendale. Mostly, though, it's for beating the crap out of the Tide, and shutting up (however briefly) the most arrogant and annoying fan base in all of sports.

It's the day each year when we take all those pent-up feelings of resentment and hostility and turn them loose on the bad guys from across the state—right there in the open, for the whole country and the whole world to see.

It's a game that makes us think back on moments of supreme transcendent joy and utter misery from years past. It's a weekend each year that makes us think of all the reasons why we despise red elephants and red polyester and people yelling, "Roll Tahd!!" It's a singular moment in time, once a year, that makes us *think*, think

131

long and hard, about who and what *we* are, and who and what *they* are, and how we are somehow the same and yet not *remotely* the same, and why.

Here are **ten things the Wishbone guys are *thinking* about** as the Iron Bowl looms just ahead:

1. Gary Danielson of CBS suggested on Tuesday that Nick Saban will be willing to do what others have been reluctant to do: put his two corners in single coverage on Auburn's receivers and bring the other nine into the box to shut down the run.

In the first place, we have to believe that Cam has developed his skills as a passer this season to the point that teams that disrespect his arm will be made to pay the price. Secondly, we're not convinced that nine Alabama defenders in the box will be enough to stop our running game, anyway—at least, not every play.

This chess match, though—the battle of minds and schemes between Nick Saban/Kirby Smart and Gus Malzahn—should prove to be supremely interesting, exciting, and entertaining. And it may well be the fulcrum upon which the outcome of the game turns.

2. It's not exactly a state secret that the **worst enemy of the Auburn offense** this season has been the Auburn offense itself. Especially during the first half of the season, the Tigers would get things going in a big way, only to have the wheels come falling off, due to false starts and holding calls and the like.

Alabama's strategy in the game will very likely include a key component of what LSU attempted to do: limit the number of Auburn's offensive possessions. With a raucous crowd at Bryant-Denny, those two factors could combine to reduce by two or three the number of opportunities for Auburn to put together complete scoring drives. This is a big part of the home field advantage that people see affecting the outcome of the game.

It is therefore of paramount importance for the Tigers to control the ball, avoid costly (and drive-killing) errors... and score when they have the opportunities to score.

The onside kick worked against them last year. It worked against Georgia last time out. Maybe it would not be out of place here, as well, in order to maximize ball control and scoring chances.

3. Re-watching last year's game this past weekend, two things in particular were glaringly apparent. First, the tackling by Auburn's defense was as good as (or better than) it has been at any time in the Chizik/Roof Era. All those missed tackles we've gotten so used to seeing this season, where an Auburn player creates a chance to make a big tackle in the backfield or in the flat, only to go flying helplessly past the ball carrier? That hardly ever happened in last year's Iron Bowl. We have no idea why that was so, but it was.

The other thing apparent from last year's contest was the strange metamorphosis of the offensive game plan in the second half, and particularly in the fourth quarter. Even as Auburn held a narrow lead and was trying to bring home the big upset, and with the defense playing out of its collective mind to hold Alabama in relative check, the offense went into a sort of drop-back passing shell. Time after time, Malzahn eschewed the quick-hitters and clever misdirections and simply had Chris Todd drop back and stand there, surveying the (covered) receivers. And time after time, he had to run for his life (and/)or be sacked.

Perhaps Alabama's coaches or players had figured something out after halftime that allowed them to completely disrupt all of Gustav's brilliant plays from the first half. Or perhaps not. In any case, this year we have to trust that our offense is still doing things late in the game that allow them to maintain possession and keep McElroy and Julio and company on the bench.

4. Alabama is a four-point favorite. Why is this so? First, home field advantage in the SEC is huge, and the crowd will be at super-intensity level from warm-ups on through the game. Second, Alabama is a very good team, one that would beat almost any other team in the nation it played. They are a complete team—solid in every area—with a defense similar to LSU's and an offense like that of South Carolina or Georgia. The difference between this year's Tide squad and last year's edition is the lack of those All-American type players who took them from *solid* or *very good* to *great*. Mark Ingram hasn't been as effective this year and the defense really misses Cody and McClain. As a result, on offense they've shifted their focus to the pass. Last year, Alabama ran the ball for 54% of its total yards. This season they have run for only 42.5% of their yards. What with Auburn's infamous weakness in pass defense, we can expect McElroy to have a big game through the air. Can we contain and limit him? A lot of bettors seem to think not.

5. If we were Bama, we would come in with two plans. The first would be to play good defense and try to establish long, ball-control drives. Even if the run game isn't working the way they might like, a flurry of four- and five-yard passes that stay in bounds, mixed with some runs, will move the ball and keep the clock running. However, if the Tide defense cannot stop our offense and we are moving the ball well early in the game, Bama will have to trash this idea and start attacking on offense with McElroy throwing the ball downfield and all over the place. (This is the role the Auburn offense plays in helping our defense in every game, through the pressure put on the other team's offense to perform and keep pace.)

6. The first key to the game for Auburn: Get pressure on McElroy. And the good news is: Alabama is bad at protecting him. Bama is *tenth* in the SEC in sacks allowed with 2.5 per game - and that includes games against Georgia State, San Jose State and Duke. Good defenses have gotten pressure on McElroy, with LSU defensive tackle Drake Nevis practically *living* in the backfield when the Tide visited Baton Rouge. Nick Fairley and company must get pressure on him and disrupt the Bama offense. It won't happen every play, but it can happen often enough that Bama will have possessions end in punts and therefore not be able to keep up with Auburn's offense in the scoring race.

Will the suspensions of Goggans and Blanc hurt Auburn? It would nice to have them, but the defensive line will not suffer too much of a drop-off. The freshmen defensive linemen have played great when they have been in the game this season and we feel very comfortable sending out Lemonior, Whitaker and Carter more than usual in the first half. Meanwhile, we expect Nick Fairley to put on a show. It won't quite be the "eleven sacks of Brodie Croyle" game, but we should nonetheless be treated to the sight of McElroy running for his life on numerous occasions. And yes, Julio Jones will hurt us, but he is not as explosive as A.J. Green, and we survived him.

7. The second key to the game: Alabama's defense is generally unable to get pressure in the opponent's backfield, and that is a problem for them. Bama is *last* in the SEC in quarterback sacks and tackles for losses (behind even Vandy!) While you know they will play good, solid defense, they don't have the kind of defensive line that Clemson, South Carolina or LSU had. They cannot get into the backfield and disrupt plays on a regular basis, and that will give the Tigers offense time for plays to develop.

8. Alabama cannot stop the Auburn offense. They may well be able to contain it at times, but the Auburn offense has gotten stronger and better as the season has gone along; it is *much* better and more effective now than it was in week three or four. The passing game is much more advanced now. And every week Malzahn has laid a few more cards on the table for defensive coordinators to deal with (and some of those are set-ups for plays he will use this week). Note also that Auburn has purposely shown some things in games this season so that Bama will scout them, line up a certain way, and then be vulnerable to something else. Count on it.

We expect the Tide to come out heavily focused on the run, so play-action passing could lead to big results in the first half. The Auburn offensive line will open up holes, protect Cam, and stay with plays. Cam is feeling much more confident passing the ball after the last two weeks. Don't be fooled by the stats; South Carolina moved the ball up and down the field against the Tide defense and Arkansas racked up 300 yards of passing against them in the first half. LSU rang them up for 245 yards on the ground (while going for only 155 against us). Auburn will move the ball and Auburn will score points. A lot of points.

9. Bama will move the ball and score points and may even take the lead for a while... but at the end of the game, Auburn's offense will prove too dominant and the Auburn defense will make enough plays to disrupt the Tide offense just enough.

Final score?
John says: Auburn 34, Alabama 24

Van says: Auburn 37, Alabama 31

10. BEAT BAMA. Bring the hate! It keeps us *oh so* warm...

24-7 Alabama at the half.

28-27 Auburn at the end.

A comeback for the ages.

But—no chance to sit back and rest on their laurels—not for these phenomenally resourceful and resilient Tigers.

The SEC Championship Game awaited them in less than a week.

Steve Spurrier—arguably the greatest living coach in SEC history—awaited them.

South Carolina, a team the Tigers had struggled to defeat in Jordan-Hare a few weeks earlier, awaited them.

Destiny awaited them...

Gravy, Destiny, and Chicken *a la* Dome

So here we stand, midway between the Iron Bowl and the SEC Championship Game. A proper respect for the historical weight of the events we have just witnessed, as well as those we may be about to witness, requires of us a thoughtful and analytical overview.

Forget that!! All we really want to do is jump up and down and run around in circles and *scream*.

We won that game. We *won* it. No, really. Even now, days later, that fact is only beginning to seep down through our skulls and into the depths of our orange-and-blue brains and actually register as fact. It seems so impossible, so preposterous. Yet it's true. From 24-0 to 28-27. *We won.*

What more can be said about the events of November 26, 2010? And what can we conjure up that will tell us how things will play out on this coming Saturday? And finally, how did we get from the depths of 2008's misery to where we are now, with two gleaming brass rings in sight (and an Iron one already in our pocket)? The Wishbone is here to address those questions.

Part I: The Meltdown in T-Town

It is an overused word in our society, but that win was truly *epic*. It really was one of the most dramatic, amazing comeback wins in SEC history—and that is even before you consider the stakes that were on the line for Auburn and the rivalry nature of the game. It was a contest that will go down in history, for a number of different reasons.

The defense was awful in the first quarter and was chewed up and abused by Alabama, but they held it together and did not quit. We can't say enough about that. It was typified by the now-celebrated play by Carter, chasing down Ingram and poking the ball loose—that miraculous ball that rolled as if it were round, as if Les Miles had designed it that way, all the way down the sideline and out the back of the end zone.

Then there was Nick Fairley, shaking off the worst officiating judgment call in SEC history and making plays again and again. And T'Sharvan Bell knocking away passes and then getting the big sack on McElroy late in the game, displaying amazing effort.

Speaking of the Auburn defense: this might be insane, but the suspensions helped us. Blanc and Goggans were fresh after halftime and helped to slow the Alabama offense. They didn't make a ton of individual plays but they were involved and were going against guys who were tired.

Alabama famously came out fired up and emotional to start the game, but they blew way too much of their energy in the first quarter. They were like a marathon runner who sprints full-bore out of the gate and then can't finish the race. It made for a truly frightening effect at first—they were a basketball team that was seeing every shot they made go in, from everywhere on the court. But they were spending too much energy dancing and celebrating, and that took a lot out of them—probably more emotionally than physically, in fact. So they eased off the throttle... and then it was too late.

Two things that have been true all season really shone through in the game for Auburn: Leadership and in-game coaching adjustments.

To be down 24-0 in the most hostile atmosphere that any college team will face this season, and given the way things were going, most college teams would have thrown in the towel. They would have wilted under the pressure and the vitriol. They would have said, "It's just not our day." But this Auburn team has a core of strong leaders. The seniors have been through so much, and they held this team together and led by example. They kept a positive attitude and tried to come back one play at a time.

Gus Malzahn has been coaching his system for so long, not only does he know it backward and forward, he knows what other coaches and teams are likely to do to try to stop it. Once he sees what you're doing, he knows your weaknesses and how to adjust in order to exploit them.

A simple example: Early in the game, Alabama was using the defensive ends to keep containment while clogging up the middle. This was effective at both stopping Cam's and Dyer's usual runs up the middle and also stopping McCalebb's sweeps to the outside. Malzahn countered this by having Cam fake the handoff to McCalebb and then clearly show he still had the ball behind center; this caused the DE to release McCalebb and attack Cam. Cam then neatly threw the ball over the DE's head to McCalebb. After two or three of these plays went for around ten yards each, Alabama had to change its approach.

On defense, Roof has taken a lot of grief this year, but during the games he has been one of the best two or three coordinators in the league. In every game, Auburn has improved after halftime. The Auburn defense dominated Alabama after the half on Friday, to the tune of allowing barely sixty yards of offense. Roof has brought more and more pressure as the season has gone along, and it clearly has made an impact. It wears opposing offenses (and quarterbacks!) down over the course of time. The return of Bell and improved play by Eltoro Freeman hasn't hurt, either.

(Van needs to note one thing more, which a quick perusal of the comments thread from the Iron Bowl Game Day Post on this site will confirm: "Before the game, I put on my traditional Dameyune Craig #16 blue Auburn jersey. However—and this was the critical, *awful* mistake—I selfishly wanted to save my orange t-shirts to wear during the week, in celebration of the victory I was so confident we would achieve. Every week previous to the Iron Bowl, I had worn an orange t-shirt under my jersey. This time, I went with a white one. We all know how the first half went. At halftime I frantically dashed into the bedroom and switched out an orange t-shirt under the jersey. And we all know how the second half went. So—I apologize for the first half, and as for the second... *You're welcome!!*")

Part II: A Coronation in Atlanta??

In the eighteen previous SEC Championship Games, there have been only *five* rematches of two teams that previously faced one another during the season. The team that won the first time is 4-1, with the only revenge-getter being LSU in 2001. (Auburn participated in two of those rematches, experiencing it both ways— we lost to Florida twice in 2000 and beat Tennessee twice in 2004.)

When Steve Spurrier took Florida to its (and his) first appearance in the SEC Championship Game in 1992, they faced an undefeated team from the West. Despite playing a good game, Spurrier's side lost. He has no magical, mystical lock on the Dome. He's human, he's mortal. A darned good coach, yeah, but mortal.

Yes, South Carolina finished the season strong. But let's be honest: playing well against this year's Florida squad (in a game of monumental consequence for the Gamecocks), and then trashing Troy and Clemson is not the same as finishing strong against Georgia and at Alabama. Don't be overly fooled by Carolina's recent run.

There is little doubt that both teams will play better on Saturday than they did in the September matchup. We cannot count on Carolina to turn the ball over four more times. Hopefully, Auburn won't kill two drives with costly fumbles again.

Speaking of which: Auburn had the ball twelve times in the previous matchup with the Gamecocks. Let's break those possessions down. Seven times, the Tigers scored a touchdown or attempted a field goal. Of the other five possessions, they fumbled twice, punted twice and let the clock run out at the end of the game. So South Carolina actually stopped Auburn a less-than-stellar *two* drives out of *twelve*. This kind of statistic is what we call *promising*.

South Carolina's pass defense has been a weakness all year. In the earlier matchup Auburn was not yet clicking in the passing game. We should expect more big plays from the Tigers in that area on Saturday.

Of course, Carolina's passing game is pretty darned good, too. They give up the sacks, but when Garcia is able to get the ball off, he has some great targets. We all know Alshon Jeffrey is a stud. We know he will get his 175 yards and two touchdowns, just as Green and Jones and the others have against us this year (mostly early in the games). The Tiger defense just has to stop everyone else— particularly our old buddy, Marcus Lattimore, who surely has to be aching for a chance to make up for his paltry performance last time. We've seen over and over that the Auburn defense can rise to such challenges, shutting down a great back and limiting the passing game of the opponent. They need to do it all over again this weekend.

It won't be a shutout. If there's one thing we know beyond question, it's that. Auburn hasn't really come close to shutting anyone out this season. This is not the 1988 or 2004 teams, winning in part by crushing the opponent's offense and preventing them from ever crossing midfield. This year's team challenges you to a tennis match and rarely has its serve broken, and gets just enough defense (and more as the game goes on) to break your serve at least a time or two. Carolina will score. Auburn will score more.

We've heard whispers of McCalebb being banged up a little. We did see Emory Blake in the sweep spot against Bama late. Losing a key component of the offense—and one not easily replaced, and one that takes a whole segment of the playbook with him—would be tough to swallow. Let's all keep Onnie Mac's legs in our thoughts and prayers this week, just in case.

Likewise, they're saying Garcia's got a chicken wing in a sling. We don't believe it. He'll be fine. Bank on it. And *bring it on*.

Part III: "Gravy" vs. "Destiny"-- Two Distinct Views on What it All Means

Your two humble Wishbone writers see this season, and Auburn's appearance in the SEC Championship Game, in contrasting ways. The two ways are very different, yet they are both distinctly "Auburn." Van takes solo voice now, in order to present John's eminently rational and logical points, and then to lay out his own vision of where we are, and what we need to do:

John, who is far more level-headed and calm and cool and generally far more rational than I am, makes the following points.

"To me, everything now is gravy. We have done what I wanted to accomplish—we beat our big rivals this year. Whatever else happens is just fun. After 2004 I am forcing myself to live in the moment and enjoy this team and these games.

"The worst case scenario is we go to the Orange Bowl and play Florida State or Virginia Tech and finish in the top five nationally. That ain't bad.

"And Tony Barnhart thinks that even if we lose to South Carolina on Saturday, we could go to Glendale anyway."

Thus spoke my great and good friend, John. And, you know, nothing he says here is wrong. His view of our season is absolutely correct, within itself. We *have* accomplished everything we could have dreamed of accomplishing—heck, even more! Who dared hope that we would not only defeat the mighty Tide in Tuscaloosa, but do it in such a way as to send them spiraling down into the depths of slack-jawed and incredulous misery? Who imagined we'd be sitting at 12-0, and with a quarterback who represents (extracurricular matters notwithstanding) possibly the biggest shoe-in for the Heisman Trophy in history?

No, nothing John says there is incorrect. And yet I could not disagree with him more.

Here is why.

Auburn pursuing a national title this season is *not* a pleasant afterthought. It is *not* the cherry on top of an already delightful sundae. It is most certainly *not* a cute little add-on to an already successful season. While taking nothing whatsoever away from what our amazing and courageous and resolute team has already managed to accomplish, the national championship is absolutely and unequivocally *critical* this season.

It is nothing short of the endpoint of a long and arduous and most holy crusade—a crusade that has covered not just one year or even one decade but over a half-century of futility and frustration.

This is why, come Hell or high water, *I will be there in Glendale* if the Tigers play for a national championship on January 10. I've traveled too far, seen too much, and been disappointed—bitterly, *bitterly* disappointed—far too many times, to do otherwise.

Like some epic quest to throw an evil ring into a fiery mountain, I must see this through, no matter what. A trip to Glendale for Auburn this year would not simply represent the culmination of a single season's work. It's not just about 2010—not by a long shot. Seeing Auburn win it all on college football's ultimate stage in January would be the crowning achievement of a very long journey—in truth, a *lifetime's* journey.

In my four-plus decades on this earth, and as an Auburn man, I feel as if I've seen it all—and seen my team denied the ultimate prize in every way imaginable. I lived through shocking outrage in 1983 when Miami jumped us (from two spots further back!); through the Ambush in Knoxville just after we reached AP #1 in 1985; through the Earthquake in Baton Rouge in 1988 that denied us an inevitable matchup in the Sugar Bowl with Notre Dame for the title (and don't you know Lou Holtz was relieved to be facing West by golly Virginia instead?); through a preseason #1 in some magazines in 1990 that evaporated into the breeze so quickly; through an undefeated season out of nowhere in 1993, that led exactly nowhere because of probation; through a 21-points-down-early comeback that fell just short against Alabama in 1994, ending the chance for back-to-back undefeated seasons; through stratospheric pre-season expectations in 2003 (the Four Horsemen of the AuPocalypse!) that fell so quickly to earth at Grant Field, among other crime scenes; and of course the granddaddy of all Auburn disappointments, stuck in third place all season long and knowing—just *knowing*, week after week, because we are Auburn and because that's what happens to us, every time—that neither team ahead of us would lose.

With notable exceptions, in order to win a national championship, a program must do one of two things: It must either be extremely fortunate in one given season, coming out of nowhere and then fading back again (as with the titles won by Georgia Tech, Colorado, BYU, and so on), or it must reach a sort of consistent "top ten" level and remain there for at least two or three years running, so that when the perfect moment presents itself, the program can surge through and grasp the trophy (as with titles won by Florida State, Nebraska, and Texas, among others, each of whom hovered for several years around the top of the polls before finally claiming a first modern-era title).

Sadly, Auburn has never quite been either of those sorts of programs. We've been too "up and down" to consistently be waiting there to pounce, FSU or Nebraska-style. And we've been too unlucky on those occasions (see above) when we could have come out of nowhere to grab a title. As they say on "Hee Haw," if it weren't for bad luck, we'd have no luck at all, when it comes to national championships.

That is why this year is so *critically* important. This team, unlike every Auburn title contender squad before it in the modern era, has seemed impervious to that traditional Auburn bad luck. They *didn't* fold up under the pressure at Tuscaloosa. There *aren't* two teams permanently lodged ahead of them in the BCS rankings. They have but to beat South Carolina on Saturday and they *are* going to play for it all.

This is Auburn's year. This is the year we banish the echoes of 2004 and 1983 and all those other disappointments. This is the year that our accomplishments, our hardware (or silverware, as the English call their trophies) finally match the historical level of our program. Alabama people will badmouth us from here till kingdom come, but we know the truth: Auburn is a national top-20 program, and deserves a modern national championship to go along with that celebrated one from 1957. As ESPN's college football guidebook stated a couple of years back, no other major program has gone longer without a national title, or is more due for one. It's time. It's *way past* time.

This is it. This is the team. This is our year. The weight of the past five decades of Auburn history rides easily on the broad and confident shoulders of Cam Newton and his mighty team.

Let's get it done.

One note of interest:

From Pat Dye's arrival late in 1980 through the graduating class of 2007, every player who spent four years in an Auburn uniform was able to claim an SEC Championship, an undefeated season, a Western Division title and appearance in the SEC Championship Game, or some combination thereof.

That streak ended when the 2008 squad failed to reach any of those goals. The failure in 2008 meant that an entire graduating class—players who had been on the roster from 2005-2008—were the first since the 1979-1982 class to leave Auburn with none of those laurels. The same held true for the next year's crop—those who played from 2006-2009. (Redshirt years notwithstanding.)

With Auburn back in the SEC Championship Game this year, that negative trend has been stopped at two years (or two graduating classes). The number of graduating classes who did not reach any of those achievements has been limited to the freshman classes of 2005 and 2006—particularly sad considering Auburn only narrowly missed appearing in the SEC Title Game in both of those years.

That was one two-year streak we're very happy to see the tail end of.

Prior to 2010, the Auburn Tigers had won the SEC football title only six times in history. Five of those titles came during or after the Pat Dye era (beginning with the 1983 championship). Only one of them (2004) came during the time of two divisions and an SEC Championship Game.

To say Auburn was due *is a vast understatement. To say Tigers fans were* hungry *is a vast understatement. To say a seventh title meant a tremendous amount to the program and to all of its supporters is a vast, vast understatement.*

And yet... and yet...

By this stage in 2010, everyone understood that the Auburn Tigers were on the verge of playing for something even bigger—something the Tigers had only ever claimed once in their entire 118 years of football on the Plains. The possibility of a national championship lay just ahead, if only the Tigers could seize the opportunity.

And so, just as in 2004, celebrations of conference accomplishments were muted by larger concerns. Would we make it into the BCS Championship Game? Unlike in 2004, this time it looked assured, provided we defeat the Gamecocks and claim the SEC crown.

What if we lost? Could we make the BCS game even without the SEC title? Some said we could. Others found it unlikely.

The simplest solution to the problem was for the Tigers to win—to defeat South Carolina again and leave nothing to chance and the whims of fate (and poll voters).

It was in that rarified atmosphere, just prior to the game in the Georgia Dome, that the Wishbone looked back at the things that had gotten this Auburn team to the very brink of greatness...

– SEC CHAMPIONSHIP GAME WEEK, Part Two –

17

Ten Things that Got Us to This Point

As the Tigers march into Atlanta for their fourth appearance in the SEC Championship Game on Saturday (moving us into a tie with LSU for fourth-most appearances), the Wishbone takes the opportunity to gaze back over the events of the past two years, taking a hard look at ten key moments, situations, and decisions that got us to where we are now.

1. Cutting Tubs Loose.

Two years ago, Auburn was wrapping up a 5-7 season with a horrendous loss to Alabama in the Iron Bowl. Despite the bleakness of that season, however, then-Head Coach Tommy Tuberville had just the year before led the Tigers to their six straight win over the Tide, and within four years had taken Auburn to an undefeated season (and the SEC title), an eleven-win season, and two nine-win seasons. Nevertheless, the powers-that-be at Auburn decided to cut Tubby loose and move in a different direction. Auburn suffered a bit of negative press and some negative reaction from fans over this move, but could anyone reasonably argue that Tuberville and the staff he had in place two years ago could have gotten Auburn to the position it occupies today—and this quickly? Auburn was willing to make the bold move and AD Jay Jacobs acted decisively. One has only to gaze a short distance to the east to see what can happen when a program instead hesitates and second-guesses and dithers itself into a slow decay and decline. We're looking at you, Mark Richt.

2. Hiring Gene Chizik.

This was the gutsy move of all gutsy moves. Jacobs knew he had the right man after interviewing Chizik, but a lot of ADs nonetheless would have been afraid to roll the dice on a coach with Chizik's two-year resume at Iowa State. His even temperament and calm but confident demeanor has been a huge—probably critical—element in this team's run to 12-0, as well as the steady hand guiding the ship through the shoals of the Cam controversy.

Of course—and we've heard this a million times if we've heard it once—*nobody* wanted Chizik at Auburn. *Nobody* was mentioning his name. *Nobody ever* could have thought that Chizik would—hey, *wait a minute!* What's this? A trio of emails that Van sent to John, the week before Chizik's name even appeared in the conversation? Hmm! Let's see what Van said:

12/4/08: John, what has Will Muschamp ever proven that would make him a great head coach? If we go that route, why not hire **Gene Chizik** *from Iowa State??*

And then:

12/5/08: And why does anyone think Jimbo Fisher would be a great head coach? Because he called plays for Saban's '03 team? Same question for Muschamp. Why is everyone so convinced he's great HC material? Why not hire **Gene Chizik***? He did just as well as Muschamp and has head coaching experience.*

And finally:

12/8/08: What about **Chizik***?? Why is no one mentioning him? He was such a hot property when he went from AU to Texas and won like 30 games in a row, from 2003-2006!*

Clearly Van is a genius. Unlike this guy—a **beat writer from ISU**, who wrote the following on December 13, after Auburn announced the hire:

"When Chizik was hired [at ISU], I told some media colleagues in confidence that his stay at Iowa State would be three years maximum. Either he would fail miserably and be fired or he would have a little success and jump on the very first opportunity that came along to move back south. Now I must admit, even I am surprised at the bizarre turn of events whereby he failed miserably at Iowa State and still got to jump on the very first opportunity that came along to move back south. What the hell Auburn is thinking is anybody's guess. And who cares. Because it just unburdened Iowa State of its most unprepared, overmatched and incompetent head coach of the modern era."

To which we reply, "You're welcome."
(John points out that he was holding out for Gary Patterson of TCU or Paul Johnson of Georgia Tech, both of which would have been good fits on the Plains, Van admits.)

3. Bringing in a Top-Notch Staff.
Excellent recruiters, excellent position coaches, and the Mad Dr. Gustav as the cherry on top. This staff exudes confidence and energy and optimism, and they are extremely effective at everything they do.

4. Kodi Burns Showing his Class.
We all remember it. The speech before the whole team prior to the 2009 season. Wounds healed—and wounds that hadn't happened yet, pre-empted. And now every Auburn fan exults a little bit harder every time Kodi catches a pass or throws a terrific block. After he graduates, he should never have to buy his own drinks in Auburn again. He is an Auburn Man.

5. The Emergence of this Crop of Receivers.
During the ten-year Tuberville Era, Auburn had exactly *one* group of receivers that stood out—that actually looked like they knew how to run routes and catch passes and block. Obomanu and

Aromashodu and Taylor and Mix: they all came to Auburn together, at the start of the 2002 season. They went on to form one of the key ingredients in the 2004 juggernaut, and were pretty much the backbone of the offense (along with Kenny Irons) as seniors. Want to know how good they were, and how important a competent WR corps can be? Compare Brandon Cox's junior year, throwing to *that* squad, to his senior year, when most of them were gone. Yeesh.

Now look at what we thought we had at receiver in 2008, and compare it to last year and this year. Darvin, T-Zac, Kodi, Blake, and the *Swede Killa*... Yeah. You see the point.

6. A Senior-Laden Offensive Line.
And the results when they are challenged and they respond.

7. The Experiences of 2009.
Last season was enjoyable and satisfying in its own right in so many ways, exceeding most fans' expectations for Chizik's first year on the job. It also served to lay solid foundations for this year's squad, enabling it to reach higher and to achieve loftier goals than nearly anyone could have imagined. From important road-game experience in places like Knoxville and Fayetteville and Baton Rouge to a close Iron Bowl and a New Year's Day bowl win, the team gelled. With the coaching staff coming back entirely intact and the addition of a few new pieces (one of them called "Cam Newton," another called "Mike Dyer"), not to mention the shocking emergence of a piece we already had (Mr. Fairley!), the 2009 team was the springboard, reminding us of the reverential tones with which Pat Dye used to talk about his 1981 premier squad: it gave us "something we can live on a long time around here."

8. The Emergence of Mike Dyer and Onterrio McCalebb on Offense; Nick Fairley and Josh Bynes on Defense.
And let's not forget Wes Byrum: the guy who, as a freshman, went into the Swamp and kicked the last-second, game-winning field goal over Urban Meyer's Gators—*twice!*

9. Cam2illa.
From bringing him into the Auburn Family late in 2009, to watching him develop as a simply astonishing player on the field

and a great leader and inspiration off the field, to suffering through the controversy these past few weeks surrounding his dad's actions, to finally seeing him achieve exoneration and be cleared to play—it has been a wild ride. Quite possibly the wildest ride in Auburn history, and one we will never forget. In only a short time a third Heisman Trophy will be carted into the Athletic Complex, placing Cam up there with Pat Sullivan and Bo Jackson. He will have completed his War Eagle Apotheosis.

10. The 2010 Schedule.

The way our schedule stacked up for us this year was nothing short of remarkable. Considering that everybody in the SEC plays pretty much the same teams, it's always seemed sort of goofy to us to talk about one team having a much "harder" or "easier" schedule than anyone else (one slight exception being the way Arkansas over the last decade always managed to avoid playing Florida or Georgia or Tennessee and somehow ended up a half-game ahead of us for the Championship Game).

If ever a schedule could be viewed as especially favorable for an SEC team, however, this might have been the year. Everyone has mentioned that, Iron Bowl aside, Auburn got its toughest games (LSU, Arkansas, Clemson, South Carolina, Georgia) at home. Beyond that, however, there were several other elements that really helped as the weeks went by.

It started soft and built slowly, allowing the team to come together week by week. The first road game was at MSU, before they really got going. The La-Monroe game allowed Cam a good early opportunity to air the ball out (on nearly every play!) prior to hitting the meat of the center of the schedule. Being able to rack up the points against a good Arkansas defense gave the players and coaches more confidence going into the very next week, against a great LSU defense. Chattanooga's placement between that hard center of the season and Amen Corner allowed a breather. Georgia's 3-4 defense gave the offense an early look at what they might expect from Alabama. Then the bye week between the Saturday of Georgia and the Friday of Alabama came at just the right time. And playing the Tide on a Friday gave the Tigers an extra day before their clash at the Georgia Dome. This schedule could scarcely have been drawn up more favorably for Auburn, and the Tigers took advantage to full effect.

There you go—ten things that got us here, to the threshold of history. Are there other things that could be mentioned? Certainly. Lots. (And that's partly what the Comments section down below here is for!) But those are the big ones that stand out to us. They've shaped and forged this team into hard steel and brought it to the brink of greatness.

Now—on to Atlanta!

56-17.

These Tigers left nothing to fate, nothing to chance.

They delivered the mother of all beat-downs to their SEC East opponents in Atlanta, breaking records for most points scored and largest margin of victory in the process.

Another trophy was coming home to the Plains.

Then the BCS computers and polls spoke, and what they said was loud and clear: Auburn was #1.

The Tigers were now officially West Bound—as in, headed directly to Glendale, Arizona for the BCS National Championship Game, to play a western team: the Oregon Ducks, with their frenetic, high-speed, high-octane offense.

To paraphrase Jerry Reed, we were hungry (for a title) in Auburn, and there was a crystal ball waiting in Glendale.

The Tigers were at least going to get a chance to do what they (at the beginning of the season) said can't be done...

West Bound and Down

West bound and down, 18 wheels a rollin'
A'we gonna do what they say can't be done
We've got a long way to go and a short time to get there
I'm west bound just watch ol'Bandit run
—Jerry Reed

Ten observations as we close the book on an incredible performance in Atlanta and prepare to devote our full attention to a squad of multi-costumed waterfowl from the Pacific Northwest:

1. When in living memory has an Auburn football team ever delivered such an unequivocal beat-down to such a formidable opponent in such an important football game?

Certainly not in any Iron Bowl we can remember. In the years when Auburn beats Bama, it's almost always by fewer than ten points, and even in the years when Auburn takes a commanding lead part of the way through the game, the Tide always manages to come back and make the final score closer than it should be.

A handful of Iron Bowls in recent years have featured the Tigers playing for something greater, and in each case they had to come from behind or hold on for a narrow victory. Beating the Tide in 2000 to get to Atlanta came down to three field goals in the muck.

Beating them for the same outcome in 1997 required a miracle last-minute fumble by Ed Scissum. In order to take them down in 1993 to finish off a perfect season, the Tigers had to rally heroically from fourteen points down.

Other big, meaningful Auburn wins, where something huge was on the line? Our wins in the 2004 SEC Championship Game and the Sugar Bowl that same season both threatened to turn into blowouts, but in both cases the Tigers put on the brakes in the second half and witnessed a beaten foe come roaring back to make the margin far closer than it had any business being.

Even our win in the 1983 Sugar Bowl—a game during which players and fans believed there was at least a chance that Auburn could claim a national championship with a positive outcome in the game—came with the Tigers kicking a last-second field goal to claim a 9-7 victory. Not enough to impress voters into moving us up from #3 to #2 in the final poll, much less #1.

So, to answer the question: When was the last time Auburn won so decisively in such a big game, with so much on the line? The only answer we can come up with is: NEVER. This team is truly special.

2. Auburn has this season already defeated teams that are appearing in the Sugar Bowl, the Cotton Bowl, the Capital One Bowl, the Chik-Fil-A Bowl, the Gator Bowl, the Liberty Bowl, the Compass Bowl, and the Meineke Car Care Bowl. *Eight* bowl teams, including a BCS bowler and several other January 1 bowls. Even the 1983 squad, famous for its 11-1 record against the toughest schedule in the country that year, would be hard-pressed to match that. And if all goes well on January 10, we can add one more bowl team to that list: BCS Championship.

3. A fast start at last. Two plays into the game, and instead of a run up the middle for no gain (hello, Iron Bowl), Cam does the little fakey-duck-down thing, then chucks the rock almost the length of the field for a huge completion to Darvin "Alshon Who?" Adams. It was obvious that Gus and Chizik understood that the Tigers needed to make a big, bold impression on offense at the earliest opportunity, to get the ball rolling and put the South Carolina defense on its collective back foot immediately. That's just what they did. *And they didn't let up.*

4. How many times this season have you caught yourself saying, "Cam Newton is even better than I thought?" Yeah. *A lot.* Us, too.

Swiper! No Swiping!

5. How nervous should it make us that Texas just fired its offensive coordinator? Is Mack Brown capable of hiring his own (successful) assistant coaches, or will he continue to try to outsource to Auburn as his Human Resources Department? Gene Chizik (also on the heels of a Frank Broyles Award) after 2004... Will Muschamp after 2007... Will yet another great Auburn assistant coach wind up moving to Austin and donning that weird brown/orange color after a big year on the Plains?

Does Gus even want to be an OC at another program—even one with the resources and the visibility of Texas? Or has he gained enough visibility and notoriety from this season to jump straight to a top head coaching job? Or does he want to continue to be in a position to innovate plays and run offenses, rather than spending so much time on the rubber chicken circuit that makes up a big portion of the world of head coaches? Would he be content to stay at Auburn for any amount of money if we win the BCS title this season? So many questions, and no answers likely forthcoming for a little while longer.

The hottest OC name right now (non-Auburn) is Dana Holgorsen, who was at Houston last year and is (for now) the coordinator at Oklahoma State. He has been mentioned at both Florida and Texas. Under Holgorsen's system, the Cowboys' offense ranked first nationally in total yards (537.58 yards per game) and third in scoring (44.92 points per game). Just as Gene Chizik went to the state of Oklahoma to grab up a mad genius playcaller (among others now on our staff) when he took the Auburn job, Florida's next head coach might well be making the trek to Stillwater to snag Holgorsen. That is, if Mac Brown doesn't grab him first. Either way, that leaves an opening that either program would love to see filled by our beloved Dr. Gustav.

(Assuming that Addazio will be heading out of Gainesville with Urban Meyer's departure, we may be seeing a "victory parade" in Gainesville whether the Gators win their bowl or not.)

One downside to the BCS Title Game coming so late (January 10): Malzahn will most likely have long-since announced his plans by then. If he's leaving us, we will go to Glendale knowing he's a— you'll pardon the expression—lame duck.

Nightmare scenario: Imagine if circumstances play out such that he leaves *before* the bowl game. Now pour a bucket of cold water over yourself and pick yourself back up off the floor. It could happen.

6. The SEC this year is overflowing with juniors who are potentially high NFL draft picks. The situation is clouded because of the upcoming labor negotiations between the NFL and the Players'

Association (NFLPA). Many observers believe that a work-stoppage is a real possibility. Players must declare for the NFL Draft by January 15, and it seems highly unlikely the NFL will reach labor peace by then. If a new collective bargaining agreement can't be reached, the current deal will expire March 3.

Players such as Cam Newton, Nick Fairley and others (see list below) therefore will have to decide whether to go pro in January or not. If they do, they may be drafted in April but could be unable to sign contracts due to the labor standoff. So they could find themselves in a situation where they don't get paid next year but cannot go back to college. Agents are probably telling these players and their families that it won't be a problem, but it should be a real concern.

Here are the SEC players who in a normal year would be giving much consideration to going pro:

Auburn: Cam Newton, Nick Fairley
Alabama: Mark Ingram, Marcel Dareus, Julio Jones
Arkansas: Ryan Mallett
LSU: Patrick Peterson
Georgia: J. Houston, A. J. Green
Florida: Janoris Jenkins
Kentucky: Randall Cobb
Ole Miss: J. Powe *(already declared for the NFL)*

At this point college players can request an opinion from the NFL advisory committee. This will give them an honest opinion at this point about where they could be drafted, to help them make the decision. We expect all of these players to request that review.

7. Auburn vs. Oregon: epic battle. Aubie vs. Puddles the Duck: Possibly even more epic battle.

8. Oregon's toughest opponent this season was BCS #4 Stanford, now bound for the Orange Bowl to face Virginia Tech. We're thinking not many folks in our part of the country got to see that matchup, but it's very instructive in helping to understand how the Ducks can just lurk and hang back and then suddenly (often somewhere during the third quarter) just explode on you—even if you are a very good team. You have them down by two touchdowns and then suddenly you realize it's *you* that's down double-digits, before you could even catch your breath. (Speaking of catching your breath, one Tennessee player reportedly told an Oregon player during the first quarter of their game in Knoxville that if the Ducks didn't slow down on offense, he was going to throw up—to which the Oregon player replied with words to the effect of, "Just wait till you see how fast we go in the *second* half!")

Stanford had Oregon down 21-3 early, and lost 52-31. That's a 49-10 swing.

Tennessee had them down 13-3 late in the second quarter, and lost 48-13. That was a 35-0 run by the Ducks in the second half.

Of course, the whole concept of big points-exploding comebacks sounds somewhat familiar to Auburn folks. We've seen it time and again this season, ourselves. Somehow, though, the way Oregon does it—so steadily, so smoothly, so relentlessly—is disconcerting. What we did to Arkansas in the last few minutes of the game? That's what Oregon does to most of their foes every week.

9. Preparing for the pace of Oregon's offense is the biggest challenge when facing them. During the regular season, there's virtually no way to get ready for it—to have the chance to thoroughly examine it and have the scout team run something even approximating it during practices. A week is simply not enough time for that dramatic a change in scheme. But... thirty-seven days is plenty of time. While there's no way the scout team could come close to duplicating that ridiculous pace, we expect that they will be running plays as fast as humanly possible—is every eight seconds too much to ask for?—in practice from now until January 10. The Tiger defense will have a lot more time than the average team did to adjust to what they will be seeing in Glendale. This represents a real benefit for Auburn.

10. Are we ready to play a team that will actually be in a hurry to put our offense back out on the field again? Does Oregon's entire approach play right into our hands?

Seemingly every team the Tigers have faced this season has attempted to slow the game down and keep Cam and Company on the bench. Limiting Auburn's possessions and Cam's touches of the ball has been Goal #1 for our opponents—though few have been terribly successful at it. But it's what we've gotten used to, for better or worse.

Now we're looking at a team that likes to measure the time it takes to drive down the field and score in picoseconds. Do the Ducks really want to keep putting our offense back out on the field that often? Do they think we can't match them, score for score? Will we speed things up in response, or try to slow it down ourselves?

They don't mind falling behind early as a result of that style of play. It doesn't faze them in the slightest. They know that a point will come—often in the third quarter, for some reason—when the dam will break and they will flood their opponent with scores.

The problem they face with Auburn is that they may not be able to pull away at any point. Just as Arkansas found when they tried to outscore the Tigers, they might late in the game be congratulating themselves on scoring 43, only to look up and see a big 65 has been hung on them.

What will they do if they can't stop us from scoring? What will we do if we can't stop them? Who will crack first? Who will come up with the key adjustment? What will we do when we have to go to the restroom but don't dare look away for an instant?

That kind of strategic thinking, on both sides, is a major part of why this game is so fascinating and so compelling. Thank goodness we have over a month to go before they meet on the field; it'll take us that long just to begin to consider and sort through all the possible permutations.

One thing's for certain, when these two take the field: *Don't blink.*

Oregon's celebrated and clever play-calling cards got the Wishbone treatment earlier in the season.
But let's be honest: As soon as they learned they'd play Auburn, the Ducks knew the score.

During the long layoff between the SEC Championship Game and the team's flight to Phoenix for the BCS title game, a number of stories made the rounds in the press. One was that Vanderbilt had offered Gus Malzahn $3 million a year to be the new head coach of the Commodores.

After a day or two of this talk, word surfaced that Gus had told Vandy, "Thanks but no thanks." In return, Auburn gave him a raise, bringing his overall compensation into the neighborhood of $1.3 million—not bad for an assistant coach who's not even the "assistant head coach." (That was Trooper Taylor.)

While the talk was flying around, however, your hard-working Wishbone columnists formed a two-man search committee of their own, looking for a likely successor, should the "Gus Bus" depart the Plains...

If the Gus Bus Departs: Finding a New OC

Gus Malzahn has made an obvious and tremendous difference at Auburn. Coming on the heels of some of the worst offense Auburn has ever seen, Malzhan installed his system prior to the 2009 season and it made an immediate impact. (Anyone that can take the leftovers from 2008, add Chris Todd to the mix, and then proceed to rewrite portions of the Auburn record books has definitely made an impact!) When that extra ingredient of Cam Newton was injected into the Malzahn offense this season, it went from great to one of the best offenses in the history of college football.

And, inevitably, due to the amazing success of this year's Auburn offense, Gus Malzahn has become a hot commodity in college football coaching searches. Schools are looking for coaches that will be successful on the field and will also help sell tickets—and Gus has demonstrated the potential to do both.

Obviously, from the perspective of an Auburn fan, we don't want Gus Malzahn to ever leave. We're ready to stage one of those phony third world elections and declare him "OC for Life." But why should he consider going now? Let's look at it from his perspective. His profile will never be higher than it is right now. He is coordinating an offense that dominated the SEC, set all-time records in the conference title game, and is now preparing for the

BCS National Championship game. His offense produced a Heisman Trophy winner and a very successful individual season for many of the players. Sometimes you have to strike while the iron is hot.

The other side of the coin is that if Gus remains at Auburn—if he chooses to be picky about job offers—he could look like less of a genius a year from now. Having Cam Newton at quarterback and four seniors on the offensive line made this team dominant. Without those players (if Cam goes pro, which we expect him to), Auburn's offense will struggle at times in 2011. If Malzahn stays, Auburn's offense should be better than 2009 but not nearly as good as this season. And if the offense regresses a little bit, or at least doesn't ring up quite as many big numbers or look quite so flashy, will the lucrative job offers still come?

Then again, Will Muschamp just got hired by Florida after a 5-7 season at Texas, because the Jeremy Foley and the Gators remembered how good he was before this season. Our own Gene Chizik famously was hired after a 5-19 career at Iowa State, because Jay Jacobs could see beyond that superficiality to his tremendous track record in previous years at Auburn and Texas. The lesson here is that one or two bad years on the recent record of an otherwise sterling resume do not constitute deal-killers. Hanging around Auburn for another year or two, at least—even if the offense takes a step or two back—could prove a virtue rather than a problem for Malzahn, particularly with regard to waiting for just the right job to come open. (After all, how much longer will Bobby Petrino stay at Arkansas? It is Bobby Petrino we're talking about—hasn't he already topped his previous record at one location?)

But, for the sake of argument, let's just say Gus does accept a job elsewhere (if he hasn't already—these things tend to move *slow slow slow FAST!*), what are Auburn's options?

Whenever the issue of a new coordinator at Auburn comes up, it's always helpful to look at the numbers. You may have an opinion about who you like or don't like, but if someone's offense or defense is consistently ranking in the top 15 in the nation, they are doing something right.

Unfortunately for Auburn, many of the offenses appearing in the upper echelons of the NCAA rankings this year are actually "coordinated" by the head coach himself—and the chances of almost any of them accepting a demotion to OC at Auburn are virtually nil. Chip Kelly at Oregon, Bobby Petrino at Arkansas, and Rich Rodriguez at Michigan are examples of this phenomenon.

So what options remain for Auburn? In general terms, the Tigers can do one of three things:

1. Promote from within.

Most Auburn fans, as soon as I wrote that, thought of the awful 2003 offense, co-coordinated by High Nall and Steve Ensminger, and so nicknamed "Nallsminger." Nothing with the nickname "Nallsminger" ever had a chance of being good, and indeed it was a train wreck. Those guys took a team with three future first-round NFL offensive players (Ronnie Brown, Carnell Williams, and Jason Campbell) and produced an offense that didn't score a touchdown until three weeks into the season!

However, all offensive coordinators started out as something else. It is very possible that one of Auburn's offensive coaches could step in and perform very well as offensive coordinator. If he has been working side by side with Malzahn for two years, taking notes every day, studying and asking questions, could this hypothetical assistant run the offense? Perhaps. One of the key lessons of 2003 is simply this: Some people have a gift for calling plays and some people do not. Malzhan has it. Bobby Petrino has it. Steve Spurrier has it. Not many others do—not to that level of accomplishment.

2. Hire a "Malzahn Disciple."

But—*is* there such a thing? Unlike coaches who have long track records of success across the top division of football, Gus hasn't really had the opportunity to develop a group of apprentices and hangers-on who fundamentally understand how to run this scheme.

If Auburn did promote from within, a loyal assistant who has helped Auburn to reach this lofty plateau while helping to run Gus's offense would be rewarded. And the Tigers would at least be trying to maintain continuity in the offensive scheme.

However, Malzahn *is* the scheme. He has been coordinating this offense alone for over ten years. He doesn't even have a paper play sheet on game day—he carries it all in his head. He implicitly understands what a defense is trying to do to stop him, allowing

169

him quickly to make great adjustments. Someone who has not been in that role, with this scheme, could not do that.

The first place we looked for a possible Malzahn disciple was back at Tulsa, where Gus ran the offense (to much success) in 2007 and 2008. The current OC there, Chad Morris, is in his first year, and the Golden Hurricane has blown up and down the field the way it did under Gus. However, he's only been on the job for a year; last year he was a high school coach in Texas (albeit one who won three state championships). He is said to be on the list of candidates for the job at Texas. We certainly think he's worth keeping an eye on.

At Auburn, the graduate assistant for offense is a guy named Rhett Lashlee, who is from Arkansas. If anyone could be considered a Malzahn protégée, it probably would be him. He coached at Springdale H.S. with Gus from 2004-2005 and went with Gus to Arkansas in 2006, as the graduate assistant on that staff. However, if Malzahn leaves, we would guess that he would take Lashlee with him to help install his system at his new program.

[Note: Lashlee accepted the position of OC at Samford in late December 2010. We consider this a good thing: he will gain the seasoning he needs as a coordinator at a small program and thus be prepared to step into bigger shoes down the road, should that opportunity present itself.]

3. Hire a new offensive coordinator from outside, preferably running a Spread offense.

This begs the question—is it really the Spread itself we like, or just the results Gus has gotten while using it? If a coach as brilliant as Gus came along and ran, say, the Run & Shoot or the Single Wing to similar effect, wouldn't we embrace that, too?

But sticking with the Spread concept here, who are the leading candidates?

Dana Holgorsen of Oklahoma State has been the trendy name of late. Will Muschamp is surely eyeing him from his new perch in Gainesville, and ol' Swiper himself, Mac Brown, would probably also relish bringing the OSU attack to Austin. We know Pitt already inquired about making him their new head coach.

Boise State's Bryan Harsin is on the ascendance, and there's David Yost at Missouri and Phillip Montgomery at Baylor, not to mention Justin Fuente, co-OC at TCU (who had a surprisingly good offense to go along with their always tough defense this season). These are guys who are well respected and whose teams are very productive on offense.

Steve Addazio is of course available. Hahaha. Just kidding. We threw that one in for our Gator friends out there.

One school that jumps out on the list of top offensive squads is San Diego State. Aaaaand hello, Al Borges. Glad you're doing well, Al, and thanks ever so much for 2004. But... um... *no.*

Rich Rodriguez has an OC named Calvin McGee. He was at West Virginia with Rich Rod as well, and the offense has not been the problem at Michigan. The rumor mill says that Florida talked to him before Meyer retired. Another to keep an eye on.

Finally, there is the (upcoming) enemy: Oregon. Their titular OC is Mark Helfrich. He coached at Boise State and Colorado and is now in his second season at Oregon. The rub is this: being OC at Oregon is like being OC at South Carolina under Spurrier, or being DC at Alabama under Saban—yes, you have the little plaque on your door that says, "Offensive Coordinator," but everyone and their mama knows who it is that's really running that phase of the game. And even if you *are* some sort of genius, you are never going to get a lot of the credit for it, because everyone already thinks your boss is the reason for your success, not you.

A Surprise Option 4!

As we were wrapping this column up today, word came along that Gus has rejected the Vanderbilt offer and will remain at Auburn, at least for now. Of all the offensive coordinators Auburn could have, "Gus Malzahn" is a clear #1 on our list, so this represents the best possible outcome we could have seen.

Beyond that, though, is the fact that now he can (presumably) devote all of his time to preparing for the BCS Title game, without having his attention divided between the Tigers and some other team whose reins he would be preparing to take up. The thought of our team coming up short in Glendale because part of Gus's brain was already in Nashville (or elsewhere) was almost too horrifying to contemplate. Imagine losing the game not because of failure, but because of our own success on offense backfiring and causing our top coordinator to be distracted. Yeesh.

So hopefully we can all just file the above list away for at least another year, and continue on with the man who is simply the best in the business. That's the way we wanted it all along.

So Gus was safely back in the orange-and-blue fold, at least for the moment. And the Big Game in the Desert was still over a week away. With New Year's Eve looming, John and Van were free to turn their attention, at least momentarily, to the other SEC-related bowl games of the season. As you will see, their insights were not what you might call "genius-level" in every case.

And even with all those other bowls lined up in the foreground, the Wishbone boys couldn't resist discussing the larger issues of Auburn in the title game—and singling out the contributions of one particular Tiger toward making the season happen...

– NEW YEAR'S EVE –

Bowls, Polls, and the Promised Land

The Wishbone is back after a nice holiday break, and rarin' to go. This week we look at a variety of topics that deserve some scrutiny; next week it's full speed ahead to the BCS National Championship Game!

Part One: Appreciating Mount Kodi

There is a player on the 2010 Auburn football team who has been involved in almost every big play of the season. He was a highly recruited quarterback coming out of high school—one of the top five in the nation to come from that class, in fact—and his commitment to Auburn was a big deal. That player, of course, is... Kodi Burns.

Kodi's unselfishness after Chris Todd was declared the starting quarterback in the fall of 2009 set the tone for the championship-caliber team Auburn has fielded in 2010. When a leader is unselfish and gives so much of himself, those around him find it much more difficult to be selfish themselves. Kodi could have transferred... he could have fussed and complained and pouted... he could have become a cancer on the team. Obviously, he did none of those things. Instead, he persevered. He asked to speak to the entire team and proceeded to deliver the speech that was a key building block for this season's success.

Let's put this in terms of another sport, so that it will be clearer. When a great basketball player says, "I don't need the ball, I'll just play defense against the other team's best player," what are his teammates going to say to that? Are they going to complain about how many shots they are getting? No. They will look at the class and maturity that player is exhibiting and they will possibly even try to emulate it. That is what Kodi Burns did in this case, and what he did for his teammates.

Kodi Burns did not grow up dreaming of being a wide receiver or of delivering great downfield blocks on the sweep for someone else. He dreamed of being a great SEC quarterback. And he gave that up for the good of the team. He showed tremendous character and that carried over into 2010.

Beyond the example of character he displayed, however, he also brought it on the field. If you think he didn't make much of an impact between the hash marks in 2010, you weren't paying enough attention.

The official stat line reads thusly: Appeared in all 13 games; 10 catches for 142 yards; 6 rushes for 10 yards and a touchdown; 2 of 5 passing for 42 yards and a touchdown. Decent enough numbers for perhaps the third or fourth-leading receiver on the team, sure—but, even then, we haven't seen the whole story of this season. Let's go back and look at a few turning point plays:

-- McCalebb's long touchdown run to beat LSU is justly celebrated in our collective memories already, only a dozen weeks or so after it happened. But—why did it happen? It happened, in large part, because of the blocking that opened up a pathway for Onnie Mac to blaze through. And Kodi Burns made the outside block that opened up that pathway.

-- When Cam Newton was falling out of bounds against Kentucky and, even as he was tumbling head-over-heels backward, threw the ball down the field and into a crowd, who came down with it? Yep— Kodi Burns.

-- Demond Washington threatened all season to spring a kickoff return all the way back for a touchdown, and he finally got one against Ole Miss. Why was the hole there? The hole he found had been created by a Kodi Burns block.

-- On many of the other big sweep plays and outside runs this year, Kodi has been the primary outside blocker. If you're seeing Cam or Onnie Mac moving through empty space, look around, because you're likely to see a defender on his backside or otherwise all hung up on Kodi's block.

-- During the first quarter-and-a-half against Alabama, Auburn's offense could get nothing at all going. What were the very first positive plays the offense made? Two passes down the middle to Kodi Burns. He made plays when no one else was, and gave the offense some much-needed confidence.

Kodi made play after play on the field this season. He made a huge difference overall, in many different ways, although those ways haven't always show up on the stat sheet. Honors have been showering down on the team and on several other individual players, and all are well-deserved. Even so, the impact of Kodi Burns should not be overlooked.

Part Two: Bowl Season

Auburn's opponent in the BCS National Championship Game hails from the Pac-10 Conference. You would not be mistaken in thinking that it seems somewhat unusual for our Tigers to face a Pac-10 team in a bowl. In fact, only once in history have the Tigers done so: Following the 1986 season, Auburn traveled to Orlando and defeated Southern Cal, 16-7 (in the final game of embattled head coach Ted Tollner's tenure).

Overall, the SEC leads the Pac-10 in all head-to-head matchups with a record of 62-39-5 (.608). However, over the past twelve years (1998 - 2009), the Pac-10 actually leads the SEC with a record of 11-9 (.550). Oregon is 4-4 against SEC teams all-time, but 3-0 since 2002, and with a big win over Tennessee at Knoxville earlier this season. (The other games were the 1930s and 1970s.)

Before we get to the fabled January 10 "Date in the Desert" with Oregon, however, let's look at the other bowl games involving SEC teams.

Bowls can represent many different things to different teams. They can be viewed by the players involved as the "opportunity of a lifetime" (see Auburn and Oregon), or as nice little season-ending treats for teams that struggled to reach 6-6. They can also be perceived by players as a necessary evil—as an undesirable add-on to a season that they really wish would just end.

Thus, the biggest factor in picking bowl game winners is motivation. Who wants to be there? Who feels they need to prove something? We all remember what Utah did to Alabama a couple of years ago, when the Tide phoned it in, having little interest in playing the Utes.

A few nights ago, Utah again provided an example of this. They were without their starting quarterback and were unable to get anything going on offense. Even so, they dragged an awful bowl game out, keeping the outcome in doubt far longer than it ever should have been, mainly because Boise State was not much interested in being there and playing Utah. After all, they were one field goal away from playing in a BCS bowl and having a legitimate argument for a share of the national championship.

Are there SEC teams who don't want to be there this bowl season? Should we go ahead and put them on "upset alert?" Let's see:

Dec. 30: Franklin American Mortgage Music City Bowl in Nashville, Tenn.
North Carolina vs. Tennessee
John: Tennessee's young quarterback, Tyler Bray, has played well for the Vols during the second half of the season. And the game is in the state of Tennessee. But who has Tennessee really beaten? Vols win a squeaker.
Van: Two teams that just haven't looked right all year. I'll take the SEC squad. Tennessee, 30-24.

Dec. 31: AutoZone Liberty Bowl in Memphis, Tenn.
Central Florida vs. Georgia
John: Central Florida won its conference, went 10-3 and lost close games to NC State and K-State. They are not a pushover. But Aaron Murray and AJ Green light up Memphis... Georgia, 34-24
Van: Lose this one, Mark Richt, and you'd better hang on for dear life. Might not be a bad idea to have an "exit strategy" standing by. Georgia, 34-17.

Dec. 31: Chick-fil-A Bowl in Atlanta, Ga.

Florida State vs. South Carolina
John: Two teams that lost conference championship games and probably deserved better bowl games. And both teams beat the crud out of UF. A pretty even and entertaining game. FSU sticks it to the chickens with a close win.
Van: Your brain screams "FSU" when you see this matchup, and then you remember it's not one of Bobby Bowden's old juggernauts facing Spurrier. I see a tough, hard-fought contest, with the Gamecocks grinding it out behind Lattimore. South Carolina, 23-20.

Jan. 1: TicketCity Bowl in Dallas, Texas
Northwestern vs. Texas Tech
John: This is a New Year's Day bowl... on ESPNU. If you get that channel you can enjoy it. The good news for Tommy Tuberville? Northwestern's starting quarterback was injured on November 13 and will miss the bowl game. Texas Tech, 34-24
Van: Tubby's back on New Year's Day! I have to admit, I'd love to see Tuberville knock off the Wildcats in a bowl only a year after Chizik and company did so. Guns up! (ps: *This* is a New Year's Day bowl?! Urghh...) Northwestern, 37-27.

Jan. 1: Outback Bowl, Tampa, Fla.
Penn State vs. Florida
John: I think Urban Meyer started a rumor this week that Joe Paterno was retiring. They should call this the "Both Offenses Suck" Bowl. I have no idea if Florida will show up to play or not. But Penn State is not good. Florida, 20-17
Van: A very interesting pairing of two very unpredictable teams. I think the turmoil at Florida will be too much for them to focus properly. Penn State, 24-17.

Jan. 1: Capital One Bowl, Orlando, Fla.
Michigan State vs. Alabama
John: We are SPARTAAAAAAAAAAAAAAAAAAAAAAAAAAA!!!!!!!!
(Sorry.) MSU is pretty predictable on offense and that is bad when you give Alabama a few weeks to prepare. I think it will be a hard fought, close game but Bama has too much firepower on offense. (Best Bama - MSU story? When Saban left MSU to go to LSU he told the staff, "Anyone who wants to go with me better get on that

airplane." No one got on the airplane and he went to Baton Rouge alone.) Bama wins, unfortunately.

Van: Ahh—my favorite bowl of all, because it's in Orlando over the holidays! I think the Spartans will be able to generate just enough offense to pull this one out. Alabama showed some weaknesses during the second half of the season that will be tough to fix in only a few weeks of bowl practice, while MSU has been remarkably resilient in finding ways to win. And, hey—wasn't this the bowl Saban lost in his final game with LSU? Heh... Michigan State, 27-24

Jan. 1: Gator Bowl, Jacksonville, Fla.
Michigan vs. Mississippi State
John: Michigan's defense is terrible. Think about the worst 2-3 minutes that Auburn's defense has played this season and that is Michigan's whole season, every game. So MSU will score, but can they stop Denard Robinson? I can't wait to find out. (I like Manny Diaz a lot and think he will come up with a few things, but on the other side Rich Rodriguez may be coaching for his job). Miss State, 28-27

Van: Is it just me, or is this a very, very peculiar matchup of teams? My instincts scream "Michigan" but I just don't see how the Wolverines' (lack of a) defense stops MSU. Miss State, 27-24.

Jan. 4: Allstate Sugar Bowl, New Orleans, La.
Arkansas vs. Ohio State
John: A fun game - I hope Ohio State players win a few individual awards so they can put them on eBay from the team hotel. Ohio State really wants to show it can beat an SEC team. But Arkansas' offense is great and the defense has improved this year. Hawgs, 40-24

Van: What a fun matchup this should be. And I cannot see how Ohio State will ever slow down the Arkansas offense. What the heck: Hawgs, 37-27.

Jan. 7: AT&T Cotton Bowl, Arlington, Texas
Texas A&M vs. LSU
John: This will be an ugly, low scoring contest that could come down to one crazy play at the end... and you know what that means. LSU, 21-20

Van: My instincts are demanding that I choose A&M. But I do not dare defy the awesome might of He Who Grazes. LSU, 20-13.

Jan. 8: BBVA Compass Bowl, Birmingham, Ala.
Pittsburgh vs. Kentucky
John: Pitt fired Dave Wansteddt and Kentucky suspended starting QB Mike "Does not miss against Auburn" Hartline. When you have no idea who will win, ask yourself the following: Who is the best player on the field? Answer: Randall Cobb. So: Randall Cobb, 33-24
Van: Did this bowl get lost or something? What is it doing on Jan. 8? Does anyone really care? The Wildcats bring it home, I think. Kentucky, 27-23

Want to know our thoughts on the **Tostitos BCS National Championship Game**? Of course you do! So *tune in next week...!*

Part Three: An Early Peek at 2011
Not ready yet to dig out the 2011 football schedule? After all, we have a tiny little Date in the Desert coming up soon. Why look ahead when we can just enjoy the wonder and majesty of the *now*?

Hey, we agree with all of that. But the truth is that the sport of college football will not come to a sudden and climactic end, for all time, just because our team possibly wins its long-awaited BCS title. Next season is going to happen whether we like it or not, whether we are ready to move on or not, and whether Cam and Fairley and the others come back or not. So we have to acknowledge it—and what better time to take our first peek at it than now?

The first prediction is already out at Early Bird Preview, and they have Auburn ranked fifth. This is pure, blind speculation, of course—we don't know yet how many of our star underclassmen will be back, including the Blessed Individual himself. On top of that, one of the biggest factors in ranking next year's squad is the schedule they will have to navigate. And it is not a pretty sight.

The 2011 season kicks off in Jordan-Hare on September 3 against the Utah State Aggies in the first-ever meeting of the two programs. The Aggies have been making the rounds of the big boys in the last few years, and it makes sense that they would finally pop up on Auburn's schedule. They should provide a nice opening day

181

challenge, giving the new-look Tigers a little workout before dutifully folding up.

In fact, the Tigers face only one conference foe before the month of September ends—a Sept. 10 date with Mississippi State. The week after the maroon Dawgs come to town, Auburn travels back out of conference to Clemson to pay our ACC cousins back for their 2010 visit.

The rest of the non-conference slate is pretty dismal. In addition to Utah State, the Tigers welcome Florida Atlantic on Sept. 24, and then mighty Samford (with new Offensive Coordinator and Gus Malzahn protégé Rhett Lashlee) on November 5. "Samford?!" you may well ask. "Since when does Auburn play Samford?!" Guess what? This will actually be the *twenty-seventh* meeting between the two! Yes, we find that hard to imagine, too. And perhaps even more staggering: Samford will be seeking their *first-ever win* in the series. Ouch.

You look at that slate of games and you think, "Easy sailing!" But then we move into October...and the path becomes much more difficult, very quickly. Here we go:

October 1: at South Carolina. Most of their SEC East-winning team will be back, including that receiver and that running back. *October 8: at Arkansas.* You may remember their backup quarterback, who will surely be taking over at the helm for the Hawgs—he's the guy most responsible for ringing our defense up for 43 points in our own house this year. *October 15: Florida.* Hey, at least this one is actually in Jordan-Hare! Then we go back on the road—*October 22: at LSU.* And then, for the cherry on top of that big ol' Sundae of Death: *October 29: Ole Miss*, in their recurring role as "Auburn's somewhat easier foe at the end of a horrific run of opponents."

Good gosh! Talk about a Murderer's Row; the month of October looks like a no-frills tour through Stalin's Gulag! We've known all year it was coming, seeing as how we had so many of our tougher foes at home *this* year. But vaguely understanding that is one thing; seeing it lined up on the 2011 schedule is something else entirely. Plugging in Samford at the end of that parade of horrors makes a lot more sense now.

The season wraps up with our abbreviated Amen Corner of Georgia and Alabama, with the Tigers visiting Athens on November

12, taking a week off, and then "welcoming" the Tide to the Loveliest Village on November 26—which is a Saturday again, so all you "purists" can quit your griping about Friday Iron Bowls.

So: a mostly-winnable slate of contests to start the year, then the Bataan Death March in the middle, followed by a slight break, and then the big two at the end. By Halloween, we should know just about everything we need to know about the 2011 Tigers.

Part Four: The Promised Land

Enough about the 2011 squad. Their fate is a mystery now, their future a blank slate, and rightfully so. They will write their own story, forge their own destiny, in the months to come.

For now, it's still all about Cam and Fairley and Darvin and Onnie Mac and Mike D and Kodi and Josh and Lutz and Mario and T-Zac and Blake and Wes B and of course those Big Uglies. It's all about that Date in the Desert.

In 1989, David Housel described Auburn getting to play Alabama in Jordan-Hare for the first time as "the Children of Israel entering the Promised Land," and he noted that one thing that made it so special was that we could enter the Promised Land only once.

In less than two short weeks, David Housel can be proven wrong, at least on that point. In less than two weeks, the Auburn Family will have another opportunity to enter a Promised Land—one that may not be quite as intensely, personally important as Dec. 2, 1989 was, but which will be much, much bigger on the national radar— and one that will be remembered for decades to come.

The Auburn Family will cross the desert of Arizona and, if all goes well, we will discover an oasis there in Glendale—a little bit of paradise for which we have fruitlessly searched for over five decades.

In less than two short weeks, the Auburn Family may at last enter the Promised Land. *Again.*

183

Thirty-seven days.

From the end of the SEC Championship Game to the kickoff of the Tostitos BCS National Championship Game, we had to wait thirty-seven long days.

Sure, during that time we had the entirety of the bowl season, save only our own game, to keep us occupied. But the bowls were, for the most part, blowouts and/or disappointments. So we watched and we waited, and those thirty-seven days simply crawled by.

In the meantime, we religiously followed the news coming out of Auburn, scavenging any scraps of information we could glean from the various beat reporters and bloggers and friends of friends of second cousins of the players. We wanted answers to a whole bunch of questions, some of which included:

* Would Gus receive a job offer so wonderful that he couldn't possibly refuse it? And if so, even if he remained on the staff through the bowl game, would he be so distracted by it that he somehow failed to have the offense ready on the 10th? He turned down the Vanderbilt offer and we all celebrated and he got a huge raise, but then came word of Maryland sniffing around after him, and we all realized that in the world of big-time college football, nothing is certain and nothing is guaranteed.

* Would the players be able to maintain their focus on winning in Glendale during the entire, lengthy layoff (which we may have noted already was thirty-seven days)? How would the coaches go about ensuring that the team got some down-time and decompressed, but then were back and ready to go when the time came? And—what if they ate too much Christmas dinner? Would Cam be weighted down with too much cranberry sauce, when the time came for him to perform?

* Would all of the players make their grades? One side-effect of playing bowl games in January is that one semester has ended and a new one is beginning. That brings with it the possibility of players losing eligibility due to grade issues. Rumors swirled in the days before the big 747 departed for Arizona: Two players are in academic trouble and might not be playing! We all held our collective breaths and waited, hoping...

When the chartered team plane reached Phoenix on January 3, Coach Chizik was asked, "Did everyone make the trip and is everyone eligible to play?" He responded, "Everyone made the trip." And so again we waited to see just what that actually meant.

In the meantime, we began to prepare our BCS Championship Game Preview column, looking in depth at the Auburn-Oregon matchup...

21

A Date in the Desert

It's time! It's time! At long, long last, it's finally time!
Here we go: the Wishbone's official pre-game guide to what to look for and what to fret over during the game.

1. Game Week

A barren desert plain. A big silver toaster rising semi-majestically / semi-bizarrely amid the cacti. A flock of extremely fast ducks in a variety of different colors of outfits.

These are the things that awaited the Auburn Tigers as they finally arrived in the Phoenix area on January 3. The Tigers swooped down on Sky Harbor Airport in a massive Delta 747, with the seniors happily ensconced in roomy, first class accommodations. Getting off the plane, they were greeted by hundreds of orange-and-blue-clad well-wishers, a horde of reporters, and an actual red carpet. For a few hours thereafter, fun and frivolity prevailed.

And then things got serious.

With a layoff of over a month since the Tigers last took the field in the SEC Championship Game, most of the concern centered around regaining the amazing "hitting-their-stride" form the team had exhibited in the second half of the Iron Bowl and for the better part of four quarters in Atlanta. Will the offense come out smooth and crisp right out of the gate, or will they be sluggish? When one reporter asked that very question of a certain Heisman-winning quarterback, he responded, "Which do you think? We're trying to shoot for the 'crisp' route."

We all certainly hope so. Falling behind to Clemson is one thing; falling behind early to a team like Oregon, which tends to light up the scoreboard in the final two quarters, would be catastrophic.

Those same high-scoring Ducks arrived in the desert a day earlier, and by Monday were already practicing hard and fast, accompanied as ever by their blaring musical background noise. The Tigers didn't play music at their practice; Newton told reporters, "We're hoping to create our own soundtrack."

One can imagine what such a soundtrack might sound like; perhaps it might blend a little of "All I Do is Win" with "Flight of the Valkyries" and Beethoven's Ninth. If all goes well on Monday, maybe they can throw in a smattering of "We are the Champions" at the end.

One programming note before we get into this final game preview of the season: Be prepared, Auburn fans, for the sounds of confusion coming from the homes of your Bama fan neighbors— they will doubtlessly be hurled into fits of uncomprehending madness when they first see the Oregon player with "Barner" on the back of his jersey. "I'm supposed to root for *this* guy?!"

2. Stop the Run!

Auburn and Oregon are two of the top five rushing teams in America. This game could come down to who is able to stop (or at the very least, slow down) the other side's running game. Both Auburn and Oregon are good enough at running the ball to make even good defensive teams look bad. (See LSU vs. Auburn, 440 yards, and Stanford vs. Oregon, 388 yards), so the defenses may have to play over their heads to create even an occasional punt.

What are the chances that either defense can find success? Let's look at both run-game-vs.-defense matchups.

When Oregon has the ball: Auburn has by far the best rushing defense Oregon has faced this season. But Oregon is the best rushing team in the nation. Auburn's defensive front has found success in the second half of the season by lining up before the snap and then suddenly shifting at the last instant, thereby creating confusion among the blockers about who each is responsible for. Cal used this effectively against Oregon and it contributed to their holding the Ducks to their worst output of the season.

Nick Fairley and the rest of the Tiger defense will need to get in the backfield and disrupt plays as they develop. Oregon's best offensive lineman is their center, and the Ducks had success against the best defensive tackles in the Pac-10. But Fairley should be able to make few big plays through the course of the game to disrupt the offense and kill some Oregon drives.

The fear there, of course, is that Oregon will run their offense the way Kentucky did, constantly rolling the quarterback and the action of the plays back and forth, laterally across the field and the line of scrimmage, wearing Auburn's linemen down. Substitution will be critically important to be sure our big guys can still breathe oxygen in the fourth quarter.

It makes for an interesting game-within-a-game: Auburn's defensive approach has been to wear down the opposing offense—and particularly its quarterback (and by wear down, we mean "wear directly and repeatedly down into the turf"). Late in games, this approach has usually taken its toll; quarterbacks find their timing disrupted, if not their central nervous systems. Oregon, on the other hand, loves nothing better than running a defense ragged for two or three quarters and then lighting them up as the second half wears on. So which will prevail here—the grind 'em down offense or the grind 'em down defense? This could well be the main question of the game.

The other key will be tackling in one-on-one situations—something that has not always been a great strength of the Auburn defense but which has improved over the last few games. The Oregon running backs can create big plays at any time if Auburn players are out of position or miss tackles. LaMichael James did not win the Heisman but there is a reason he was at the ceremony: He is an explosive, talented running back. He does not require his O-line to open a big hole in the defense; if he can find a crease he can slip through and be twenty yards downfield very quickly. Auburn will have to be strong at the point of attack and not let those creases develop.

When Auburn has the ball: Anyone who believes that Auburn's advantage in weight along the front line will result in the Tigers pushing Oregon around all game should go back and watch the Rose Bowl. Wisconsin outweighed TCU by more than the Tigers outweigh Oregon, but the Badgers ended up losing anyway. (We would also argue that Wisconsin's failure was the result of attempting to pass too many times.)   The best rushing team Oregon played this year was Stanford, and Oregon held them to 177 yards.

Auburn's offensive line has a size advantage, but they are also better run blockers than Oregon may have seen in the Pac-10. Auburn's linemen have faced off against SEC defensive linemen all season and the prospect of facing smaller, quicker opponents is not going to confuse or intimidate them.

Oregon's defense is the 16th best in the nation at stopping the run; they are in the same area statistically as South Carolina and Mississippi State. So running against them will not be easy.   Much the way things went in the SEC Championship game, Auburn may have to come out passing to open up the run. With so much time to prepare for a defense, you have to like Gus Malzahn's ability to examine what Oregon likes to do and create a game plan that can work—not to mention his phenomenal talent for adjusting during the game itself.

3. The Other Guy

Oregon quarterback Darron Thomas will be "the other guy" this week as the media spotlight shines directly on Cam Newton.   But Thomas is a dangerous player—his play early in the season made Oregon fans quickly forget Jeremiah Masoli, who transferred to Ole Miss because they had a great graduate program in Victorian English literature.   (Or rather, they had a desperate coach and a need for a quarterback who could make plays.)

Thomas is more of a passer than a runner.   Averaging 41 (net) yards per game rushing, he is not in the same class of rushing quarterback as Cam Newton or Michigan's Denard Robinson. So his running the ball is not a central focus of the Oregon offense, but his passing is.   Nonetheless, when Oregon needed it, he came though carrying the ball, to the tune of 117 against Stanford, 62 vs. Cal and 62 vs. Arizona. So it is not that he *cannot* run the ball, it is that he only had three games with more than ten carries. Thomas is a good ball handler and many of his runs will seem familiar to Auburn fans (such as the fake handoff to the tailback, followed by a keeper/read option to the outside).

One thing to note about Thomas: he started off great but did not finish as strong as a passer. (This contrasts starkly with Cam, who appeared to improve every single week in the passing game.) In the first nine games, Thomas averaged 230 yards passing per game. Over the last three games (against Cal, Arizona and Oregon State), he averaged 149 yards per game.

Auburn has been susceptible to good passing attacks this year; with the focus of the Auburn defense on stopping the run, Thomas could come out passing and move the ball successfully on Auburn's defense. In the "receiver who will scare Auburn fans this week" role we have Jeffrey Maehl of Oregon—definitely Thomas's favorite target and a big-game player. Maehl averages twice as many yards per game as the next best receiver for Oregon, so he will be one to watch.

4. The Cam Factor

In the SEC Championship game the Auburn offense finally unveiled the full package. Cam Newton's improvement as a passer over the course of the season has made this offense almost unstoppable. Oregon will choose to focus on stopping the run—and Auburn must exploit that fact by coming out passing. Oregon's secondary is very good—but they like to play man-to-man coverage because they blitz a *lot*.

In fact, Oregon blitzes as much as any team Auburn has faced this year—something the players became aware of (to their seeming surprise) as they watched film of the Ducks. The boys from Eugene want to get in the backfield and disrupt the opponent's offense and they will bring players from everywhere on the field to do so. This can be successful against Auburn if the Tigers' plays get broken up before they get started. However, this can also be extremely risky against Auburn because Newton is such a great broken field runner. If the ducks blitz Auburn and they miss, Newton will be taking off with the ball, and the Oregon defensive backs may be in man-to-man coverage with their backs turned to him. Make no mistake: Oregon will get to Auburn at times. They will stop some running plays before they get going, especially the slow-developing plays. (Can we all hope that, this time, Gus leaves some of his fancier and more complicated creations back in the Loveliest Village and just goes with what works best?) But if they blitz as much as they have all season, we can expect several game changing plays from Cam Newton when he breaks containment and runs. In last year's Rose Bowl, Oregon had real problems defending Terrelle Pryor—and as we all know, Pryor is no Newton.

The bottom line is this: When the game is on the line and Auburn needs a first down, Cam *will* get that first down. He will make the plays when Auburn needs it.

5. The Second Half

Both of these teams played their best football after halftime.

Oregon was amazing in the second half this season, outscoring opponents 277-77 after halftime. That is due to the Ducks' depth, their offensive pace wearing opponents down, and good coaching adjustments on both sides of the ball.

Auburn has outscored opponents 246-117 after the half. Both teams adjust well and both teams have the kind of offenses that can wear opponents down over the course of the game.

What does this mean? It means that this game will not be decided until the very end. With these two teams, no lead is ever safe. Auburn must play a complete game to win.

And so if you look up at some point in the second quarter and see that either team is winning by a sizeable margin, don't get too excited and don't panic. It won't be over till it's over.

6. Game Predictions

Oregon is an excellent football team. They range from good to great in every area (if you look at the statistical rankings of every team in college football, the worst thing Oregon does is kickoff returns (and they are only two yards worse than Auburn in that area). They are in the top twenty in almost every category. So while the offense gets all the attention and the headlines, this is a definite top five team from top to bottom. Auburn is going to have to play very well to win the game.

John: Oregon's offense is too good for Auburn to shut them down, but Fairley and company will have enough success that the Tigers can pull away at the end and win a close, high scoring game.

Cam Newton will show why he deserved the Heisman by making plays when Auburn needs them.
  Auburn 48 - Oregon 44.

Van: Many expect a high-scoring shootout, along the lines of the AU-Arkansas game; others go the counter-intuitive route and predict that one or both defenses will somehow rise up and hold the scoreline to a more reasonable sum. I think the truth lies somewhere in between. I expect the game to most resemble our clash with Kentucky back in October. Oregon is much better than Kentucky, but Auburn is playing much better than they were at that point in the season, too—so it's a wash. That game saw Auburn jump out to an early lead, then hang on for dear life as the Wildcat offense (led by a mobile, quick-throwing quarterback and an elusive ball-carrier) came roaring back to tie the game late. I envision something along the lines of this: Auburn leads early; Oregon jumps ahead before halftime; Auburn retakes the lead and then extends it into the third quarter; Oregon catches up late and forces Auburn to go on a long scoring drive to win at the end. There's no way I could ever pick against Auburn in this game, but I honestly think we are going to win. I will say:
  Auburn 45 – Oregon 42.

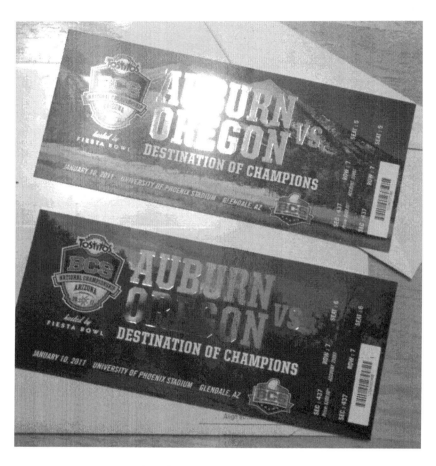

Precious, precious tickets.
Face value $300; by the week before the game, they'd be going for a minimum of $3900 each and StubHub would have to close down sales due to demand exceeding supply, while offering those who had them already a 300% refund. They would be called the most in-demand ticket in US sports history, topping even Super Bowl tickets.

Everyone who made the pilgrimage to Glendale, Arizona for the BCS National Championship Game has a story to go along with it. From outrageous ticket prices (and widespread counterfeits) to snow and ice storms grounding flights out of Atlanta, Birmingham and Montgomery, to the viewing parties on the Auburn campus being canceled at the last minute, both the weather and the economy threatened to derail the plans of many of the Tiger faithful.

Nonetheless, most of us eventually arrived, safe and sound, in the desert. And did we ever. Our sheer numbers overwhelmed the pre-planned parties and pep rallies, not to mention the Ducks fans, who found themselves in the distinct minority, even in a PAC-10 state. We bought everything in sight that was orange and blue or had a BCS patch on it, and we yelled "War Eagle!" at each other to the point that most of Arizona never wants to hear that phrase again.

We all did our best to enjoy the various sights and sounds of the greater Phoenix metropolitan area. (In Van and Ami's case, they were fortunate enough to stay with Ami's uncle's family in Scottsdale, who treated them to terrific hospitality and a wonderful sightseeing tour over the two days before the game). But let's be honest: It was tough for any of us who also belong to that other family—the Auburn Family—to devote full attention to the shops and restaurants and the mountains and desert and cacti. Like it or not, most of our thoughts were focused, laser-like, on Monday evening, and on the real business at hand.

There, in the desert, time stood still. The seconds crawled by. It began to seem as if Monday would never arrive.

And then, and then, and then... at long last... it arrived...

– THE BCS NATIONAL CHAMPIONSHIP GAME –

A Season of Our Dreams

Perhaps you've heard by now: Late in the evening of Monday, January 10, 2011, Auburn University defeated the University of Oregon by a score of 22-19 to win the BCS College Football National Championship—Auburn's first broadly-acknowledged national title in football in fifty-three seasons.

In addition, the Tigers completed a perfect 14-0 season, giving Auburn *three* undefeated runs in the past seventeen years—an accomplishment unmatched by any other program in the country.

It is now, as of this writing, a full week later... and we still don't know exactly how to react to this, or what to say about it.

By any reasonable measure, for the Tigers to have won it all this year is improbable; indeed, even in retrospect, it seems almost impossible. But it happened. It *really happened*.

Your intrepid Wishbone columnists have been struggling to come to grips with this almost unfathomable occurrence for nearly every second since Wes Byrum's kick sent the ball through the University of Phoenix Stadium uprights on the game's final play. One of us (Van) was there, in the big silver toaster in the desert, absorbing the raw emotion of the moment; the other (John) was safely ensconced with his family at home in front of the television, taking in all the

197

discussion and analysis. Together we got the complete picture...and yet, even so, we scarcely know where to begin or what to say.

We simply want to jump up and down and scream our happiness. For fifty-three more years, we want to scream.

Because, of course, that's how long it took: more than five decades. The last time people were yelling "War Eagle!" about a national championship, the other popular catchphrases were "I Like Ike" and "I Love Lucy."

It truly is mind-blowing. We find it hard to believe. It's not that we've ever bought into the propaganda emanating from the western side of the state, designed to make us feel somehow inferior, like second-class citizens (or "little brothers," if you prefer). Those people have to tear us down in order to feel better about themselves, and we understand that. It's easy to ignore, if annoying nonetheless.

Propaganda aside, though, these have been fifty-three years of incredibly bad luck for Auburn when it comes to national championships. We all know the dates—they burn in our minds with equal measures of pride in the success we enjoyed and disappointment in the greater prize we were denied: 1958, 1983, 1988, 1993, 2004.

For an Auburn team to defy all the odds, all the history, and all the bad mojo, and simply go out there to Glendale and *get the job done*... well, as Auburn people, we're in a territory just as uncharted as some of that Arizona desert we just visited. Consequently, we don't quite know how to react. Sure, we're running around and buying up all the souvenirs, all the t-shirts, all the commemorative magazines and DVDs we can find. We just can't wrap our minds around the fact that these are the real deal, and not some kind of pseudo-regional consolation prizes, as were the *Sports Illustrated* special issues we still prize in our collections (but with mixed feelings) from 1993 and 2004.

In a way, there's some of the feeling of Wile E. Coyote from the cartoon where he finally succeeded in capturing the Road Runner, after fruitlessly pursuing the little beast for what must have felt like *at least* fifty-three years to him. The Coyote held the Road Runner up, looked at us, and asked, "So, I finally got him—now what do I do with him?"

Auburn University has a BCS National Championship. We find ourselves looking around in shock and asking ourselves, "What do we do with it?" It all seems a little surreal, a little unreal.

But, hey, don't worry—I'm sure we'll figure it out before too long. We have a year to reign, and the rest of our lives to savor it afterward. That's plenty of time.

Before and During the Game

Roaming all over Scottsdale and Glendale and the immediate site of the stadium in the hours prior to the game, we encountered far more Auburn fans than Oregon fans. Indeed, the ratio ultimately appeared to be roughly 2-1 in favor of Tigers supporters. Since many past Auburn bowl trips have seen us at least marginally outnumbered by our opponents' fans, this was quite surprising and encouraging.

It was clear that Glendale was not fully prepared for the Auburn Family to descend upon them. Stores ran out of Auburn merchandise very quickly, while a good deal of Oregon paraphernalia lingered on shelves and temporary tables. Restaurants and bars overflowed with orange and blue. We were turned away from every Auburn event we tried to gain entrance to, because of overcrowding.

For their part, Oregon fans walked around with something of a bemused expression on their faces, seemingly surprised by the numbers and the fervor of their upcoming opponents. That's not to say the Ducks supporters were not in all cases as excited and passionate as we were; they simply didn't seem to fully appreciate the magnitude of the moment. We mean no offense by this; it was simply the impression we took from them. Of course, they don't have the history of "close-but-no-cigar" that we have, so it is understandable. Perhaps, now that they have their own very near miss to fire them up, they'll come with all guns blazing next time. As long as that "next time" isn't against us, we wish them all the luck in the world.

Prior to kickoff, the Oregon fans we spoke with carried themselves with a healthy amount of confidence and bravado. They had every reason to feel that way—their offense in particular had been spectacular all season, ringing up their PAC 10 foes (and Tennessee, too) with sudden deluges of points. They believed with utter conviction that no one could truly stand up to the frantic pace of their scoring machine, and they held as a received truth that Auburn's defense would, in its turn, wear down just as surely and completely as had every other defense they had faced in 2010.

Thus it was with no small bit of pleasure that Auburn fans watched their Duck counterparts slowly deflate over the course of the game, as the Auburn defense continued to mostly dominate their previously unstoppable offense. As the game wore on and the Tigers didn't wear down, confidence in the eyes of Oregon fans dissolved into concern, then into fear, then into dejection. They were sitting on eleven points for a very long time, and they were falling farther and farther behind, and the clock was ticking right along toward the fourth quarter.

And yet, for all of that, Auburn never could quite land the knockout blow that would have surely ended the game much earlier. Numerous chances came and went by the boards, and still Oregon trailed by only a single possession. One major reason why Auburn could not pull away was that, shockingly, Cam Newton was playing his single worst game as a Tiger.

A bad game for Cam is a relative thing, of course. He threw an early interception and coughed up a late fumble. (His many detractors doubtlessly felt this to be divine justice; if so, then his ultimate victory must have soured their mood mightily.) He just missed on two potential touchdown passes, under-throwing the short one and over-throwing the long one. He seemed tentative when opportunities to run presented themselves, hesitating and looking for passing lanes instead; fans had to be wondering why he didn't tear through the Ducks on foot the way he had through LSU and Arkansas and so many others. When given the opportunity to bulldoze his way into the end zone on multiple occasions, he instead found himself stood up and stopped. It was as if the Ducks had found a supply of Kryptonite and were shockingly bringing the mighty superhero to his knees.

More likely, he was simply not his usual physically-sound self. In other words, he was playing hurt—and for more of the game than most people seem to realize.

Early in the game, he took a shot that sent him spinning in the air—whereupon those of us who were looking saw why he wears that big bulky protective belt around his waist. As he spun about in the air, another Oregon player speared him in the small of the back with his helmet. A later (and more publicly discussed) collision contributed further to his debilitation. By the final drive of the game, he was doing well to throw the ball accurately and hand it to his running back.

Fortunately for all of us in this thing we call the Auburn Family, the rest of the squad stepped up. Once again we saw that this was anything but a "one-man team"—much to the surprise of the Oregon fans to our left, who proclaimed beforehand that if they could stop Cam, they would easily win. Our great quarterback was definitely a once-in-a-generation phenomenon, but he had those same largely over-achieving and under-recognized receivers and backs to pick up the slack that he's had around him all year. It didn't hurt that the back he was able to hand it to on that final drive was none other than one Mike Dyer, a compact and determined bulldozer of a runner—and one with remarkable balance and agility.

If Dyer had gotten thirty-plus carries, he likely could have finished with over three hundred yards rushing, and Auburn would have won by double-digits. We know now that Oregon had no answer for Dyer up the middle, and he still ended up with 142 yards of rushing despite not being featured until nearly the end of the game. Many of their fans hadn't even heard of him before the game—Van found himself explaining just who this mighty dynamo of a true freshman was to the Ducks sitting next to him, during the first quarter.

Of course, as always, the engine driving the Auburn attack was that great offensive line, which gave us one last fantastic performance in their final game together. Cam had a good bit of time to throw in the second and third quarters and by the fourth stanza Dyer was finding those holes in the Oregon defensive front. Indeed, it was the Ducks' smaller defense that was wearing down at the end, not the Tigers', as Auburn ran *eighty-five plays* before all was said and done. (Gus has said he's never lost a game in which he got to call as many as *eighty* plays. That's still true.)

The Defense Steps Up
What nobody really saw coming before kickoff was just how well both defenses would play—though, in retrospect, given the long layoff between December 4 and January 10, it does make sense that

the offenses would struggle while the defenses would be extremely prepared.

If, like many, you lamented during the season that this Auburn team was no longer dominating opponents with defense, then this BCS game was tailor-made for you. This was a defensive performance for the ages—and for those great units of Pat Dye and Tommy Tuberville, of Wayne Hall and Gene Chizik himself.

Nick Fairley perhaps moved himself all the way up the NFL draft charts to #1 with a world-class performance, demolishing and destroying the Oregon rushing game and offensive line. Where to begin? His constant pressure on Darron Thomas wore away at the Duck QB's performance level and led to rushed passes, a fumble (recovered by Oregon), and an important early interception. His sack of Thomas at the Auburn goal line kept the Ducks out of the end zone. His great plays in the Auburn red zone kept Oregon at bay. Perhaps the biggest single play in the game was his tackle of Kenjon Barner on fourth and goal at the Tigers one-yard line with less than three minutes to go in the third quarter.

Has a single Auburn defensive player *ever* had a bigger game on a bigger stage than this one by Nick Fairley? We think back to Aundray Bruce more-or-less singlehandedly demolishing Georgia Tech in the fourth quarter at Grant Field in 1987, turning him into the eventual #1 pick in the following NFL draft. But that game was important only if you were a Tiger or a Yellowjacket in 1987; losing it wouldn't have even kept Auburn out of the Sugar Bowl. The 1994 defense, not great against the run, put on some memorable shows against passing teams (notably Florida and LSU)—but even that astonishing, multi-interception fourth quarter to beat LSU saw the picks spread across several defensive backs, not just one player. No, in all the days since Pat Dye first made bone-crunching defense the calling card of great Auburn teams, Nick Fairley's performance might well have been the single best big-game defensive performance ever by a single Auburn player.

Of course, the entire Auburn defense stepped up and played a great game. Tackling was good, the busted assignments that Oregon thrives on were mostly avoided, and the Ducks were held to only seventy-five yards rushing overall, or 2.3 per carry—just a tad below their season average of over three hundred per game.

White Helmets, Black Hats?

Some viewers and a few journalists noted a remarkable paucity of "SEC! SEC!" chants by the Auburn crowd in the stadium after the game. Van, in the upper deck, heard only one feeble attempt break out, and it didn't last long. John, watching the TV broadcast, didn't hear much of it at all. Because this represented a fifth consecutive win by an SEC team in the big BCS game, the whole conference angle was thought to be a pretty big deal. Auburn was (theoretically) in Glendale as much to defend the honor and the dominance of the SEC as it was to win a title for itself.

But was that really true? Unlike in the four previous years, this year's representative felt all along that the rest of the conference was not terribly supportive of us. Each fanbase had its own set of reasons: Miss State (and possibly Florida) fans are mad about Cam and the recruitment scandal; Georgia fans hate Nick Fairley and have generally wished us nothing but ill in the days since we defeated them; the LSU nation has forever held Auburn as beneath their contempt. And of course Alabama is Alabama; we would be shocked and offended if they *did* find it in their hearts to cheer for Auburn under any circumstances, much less these rather unique ones.

The response on the part of much of the Auburn Family therefore was along the lines of, "The heck with them—we won this for Auburn and not for the SEC as a whole." The other powerhouses in the conference never liked us, never supported us, and certainly never believed we would win—or that we even deserved to. To them, on the evening of January 10, 2011, the Auburn Family politely replied, "Stick it."

We understand the feelings of those guys and others who want to tell the national media and the other college football fans out there that they can take their criticism of Auburn and shove it. The temptation to just unload—to shove this achievement (and the crystal football of the Coaches' Trophy) down the throats of the guys who attacked us so persistently and so viciously—is vast. In some ways, it would be enormously satisfying to just turn heel and embrace the dark side.

Maybe we're being greedy, though, but we would like to have both the National Championship *and* the good thoughts and wishes of the American football-watching public. We would like for the

203

Tigers to be thought of the way they deserve to be: as good guys, not bad guys. We'd like this collection of players and coaches to be universally loved and/or respected for the great team that they were and are. We didn't want to turn on the radio or open *Sports Illustrated* or flip over to ESPN they day after we at long-last win the BCS National Championship and have to hear or read stuff like, "How long until they have to forfeit the title?" (with a sort of relish and gusto in the delivery) or rehashes of the Cam/Cecil story or long diatribes against Nick Fairley. We don't get how those people can't see beyond the distractions and grasp just how tough minded this team was or how composed they were or how well coached they were, and just how much there was to like and admire and appreciate about them, even if you're an (allegedly) impartial journalist and not an Auburn fan. But they can't—or they don't want to.

So what we all have to admit and reconcile ourselves with and perhaps even embrace is the concept that we won it all while wearing the Black Hats. To many viewers and commentators, we have become the bad guys of college football—something along the lines of this new decade's Miami Hurricanes. Of course there is no substance to that—no reality. Quite the opposite, in fact. But the perception remains, and we cannot control it. It looks as if we have no choice but to live with it, at least for now.

And if we're dealing in perceptions, the one that really matters and will continue to matter for decades to come is this one:

A Win for the Older Folks—and for the Future

This was a win for the entire Auburn Family, obviously, but it was particularly a win for the older folks—the die-hards (not just the Dye-hards!) and the long-suffering supporters of the orange and blue. It was a win for the folks who woke up on January 2, 1984, to find that Miami had jumped us for #1. It was a win for the folks who felt the earth move in Baton Rouge in 1988 and knew deep inside that we had just stepped in front of a bullet and taken a wound from which there would be no real recovery that year. It was a win for the people who listened on radio in 1993, or who crowded into Jordan-Hare to *see* that team perform in the only way possible—with their own eyes. And of course it was a win for those who watched the weeks tick by in 2004 and embraced the wins while knowing—just *knowing*, deep inside, in a way that only a true Auburn person can know—that neither USC nor Oklahoma was going to lose, simply because we are Auburn and that is how the world works.

That's a big part of why this season we just witnessed was so amazingly, astoundingly, unbelievably *special*. Because, for once—for one time in all these years—that inevitable *something* that always happens because we are Auburn... *did not happen*.

Young people can enjoy this for its surface glitz and glamour: their team is the best in the land, and they will be and should be very happy. But those young Tigers fans won't fully understand what they've just witnessed. They haven't suffered the way the rest of us have. They haven't endured what we older fans have. They will look at this and think it is *normal*.

It was *not* normal. At least, not in the football history we have all grown up with. Perhaps, just perhaps, it will *become* the norm for the future. We certainly hope it will. Time will tell—time, and one game at a time.

In the meantime, those young Tigers fans will grow up in a different world—a world where Auburn has recently won the biggest prize of all. Perhaps they will expect more than we did from the program. Perhaps they will *demand* more than we did. Perhaps they won't be satisfied until Auburn reigns supreme.

And perhaps, just perhaps, they'll get their wish.

Bringing it Home

The 2010 Auburn Tigers did what no Tigers team in fifty-three years before them could do: They brought home the biggest prize of all. And they did it in the most improbable fashion imaginable—with a junior college transfer at quarterback and a maligned second-year coach at the helm, and with a team that very well may not have been the most formidable Tigers squad to suit up even in the past *seven* years, much less fifty-three.

Yet they did it. Despite all of the obstacles in their way, they got it done. They went out to the desert and in that barren landscape they discovered a fountain of hope and promise and boundless joy. In their labors they secured for us the blessings of ultimate victory and brought that home for the entire Auburn Family to share in, to bask in, to cherish and enjoy forever.

Now one door has closed, and another door opens.

The door at last has closed—has been slammed closed, emphatically—on fifty-three years of futility and frustration and disappointment. That long, dry segment of Auburn history is just that now: history.

A new door opens on a future that looks to be filled with promise of success and joy; a future that is very bright indeed. That door was opened by these Tigers on that night in the desert.

And for that—and for so very much more—we thank the 2010 Auburn Tigers. We thank them for providing us with a season of our dreams. And we shall never forget them. Never.

War Eagle Forever.

Wes kicks it through.

– AFTERWORD–

John says:

There are many days that one could pinpoint that led to the results we enjoyed on January 10, 2011. One of my favorite days to consider is September 19, 2009.

Why does that date matter? On that day Auburn hosted the West Virginia Mountaineers in a televised night game. Prior to the game, a massive storm system rolled in, and kickoff was delayed by torrential downpours and lightning. Many teams' fans might have packed it in for the night. Most teams' fans would have at least retreated to shelter, maybe to return, maybe not.

Auburn fans that night did not leave. Theystayed. They stood out in the rain and they sang and cheered. For hours they stayed there in the stadium, ignoring the weather.

One might ask, what possible difference could that have made in winning a national championship almost eighteen months later??

Simple. Two things happened that night in the rain. One was that the bond between that group of players and the Auburn Family was strengthened. The players saw and heard what was going on in the stands. They took note of it, and they loved it.

The 2010 Auburn Tigers and their fans enjoyed a tremendous relationship from start to finish. When the team would run down to the student section at the start of the fourth quarter of every game, the emotion passing between the team and the fans was intense and genuine. The team knew that the fans were always going to be there supporting them, giving them everything they had. The players did the same in return.

The other thing that happened that rainy night in Jordan-Hare is that prized high school recruits who were in attendance or watching the game on TV saw what the fans did, or they heard about it later. Some of those high school recruits were guys like Michael Dyer, Trovon Reed, Antonio Goodwin, Shon Coleman, and a junior college quarterback by the name of Cameron Newton. Now, was that night of singing in the rain the primary reason those players decided to come to Auburn? No, of course not. But it certainly didn't hurt.

I have always believed that Auburn has the best fans in college football. Now those fans have the best *team* in college football, too.

War Eagle!

Van says:

I thought mightily about including in this book some portion of the statistics that have been making the rounds lately, showing how Auburn has achieved the upper hand against the University of Alabama in nearly every competitive category in football in what I think of as the "modern era," or the past thirty years—a period that begins with the hiring of Patrick Fain Dye as head coach prior to the 1981 season. From overall wins to Iron Bowl wins to SEC titles to Heisman Trophies, Auburn now leads the Tide in almost every way imaginable.

But I decided against it. I concluded that this book was to be about Auburn, not about Little Brother from Tuscaloosa. They get all the coverage they need in the chapters before and after the Iron Bowl. That's plenty.

There are other eye-catching football statistics I'd love to trumpet to the heavens, but they didn't quite seem to fit into this book, either. This is as good a time as any to toss them out there. For example, Auburn in the current century (and millennium) leads Tennessee 5-0 head to head, beating them at home, away, and at a neutral site, and not having lost to the Vols since 1999, in Tommy Tuberville's first season. Auburn leads Florida in this century 3-1 (can you believe the Tigers swept Steve Spurrier and Urban Meyer, and the only loss was to Ron Zook?) and never lost to Tim Tebow. Auburn holds a 7-3 advantage over Alabama during that time and, as of this writing, the almighty Nick Saban's record against Auburn stands at 4-5. Auburn's record in this century against Urban Meyer is 2-0 and against Steve Spurrier is 4-0.

There are other points worth noting: Auburn has now won its last four bowl games, and each of the last three was won on the final play of the game: Kodi Burns ran it in against Clemson in overtime in the Chik-Fil-A Bowl; the Tigers knocked off Northwestern (multiple times) in overtime in the Outback Bowl; and of course Wes Byrum booted it through in Glendale. Auburn's bowl record this century is a sparkling 7-2, including wins over Penn State, Wisconsin, Virginia Tech, Nebraska, Clemson, Northwestern, and Oregon. None of those should be taken lightly or taken for granted. I only wish we'd gotten a shot at Oklahoma or Texas somewhere along the line—or one more go-round with USC.

There are of course other statistics from other seasons that could be mentioned and explored. But this book was not to be about those other Tigers teams—at least, not directly. And it was not to be about our rivals and other foes. Nor was it about the SEC and its fifth straight BCS title (and we all know the 2004 Tigers would have made it seven out of eight if they'd been granted the opportunity).

No, this book was not intended to be about any of that. This book was intended, from start to finish, to be about the 2010 Auburn Tigers and the season they put together for themselves, and for all of us. For the Auburn Family. The Auburn Family that we have thus far failed to point out was ***ALL IN***.

What exactly does that mean? To be honest, I'm still not entirely sure I understand it myself, even at this late date. But I have a general sense of it—of what it means, at least on an emotional level—and I know I like it.

Outside the stadium prior to the title game in Glendale, an Auburn woman volunteered to take a photo of my wife and me. As she was taking the camera from Ami, she looked at me and asked in all seriousness, "Are you *all in*?" My eyes widened for an instant. The part of my brain that is logical and analytical wanted to ask exactly what that meant. But before I could even begin to formulate such a question, I found myself grinning and replying, *"I am so far in I can't see back out."*

So even if we can't come up with some technical, rational explanation for "All In," at the gut level we all get it. We've seen (or held) those signs that read, "AU Family: ALL IN," and we get that this really has been a *family* thing, something we've all been in together, for better or for worse.

Following this team throughout this season-out-of-nowhere, and believing in its promise and its potential, required a deep and abiding faith and love for the orange and blue—the sort of faith and love one reserves only for family. For that matter, standing firmly by the Auburn program year in and year out and weathering disappointment after disappointment on the national stage has required love and faith—and has *nurtured* that love and that faith, and made those things stronger, tempering them with fire into cold steel.

The 2010 Auburn Tigers took that cold steel and used it to run through every opponent that stood in their way.

They were our family, and we were ALL IN with them. We gave them our support and our faith and our abiding and unconditional love, and they rewarded us with the biggest prize of all.

They gave all of us a season of our dreams.

Appendix One:
Auburn Tigers 2010 Schedule and Results

Sat, Sept 4	vs. Arkansas State	W 52-26	1-0 (0-0)
Thu, Sept 9	@ Mississippi State	W 17-14	2-0 (1-0)
Sat, Sept 18	vs. Clemson	W 27-24 OT	3-0 (1-0)
Sat, Sept 25	vs. #12 South Carolina	W 35-27	4-0 (2-0)
Sat, Oct 2	vs. Louisiana-Monroe	W 52-3	5-0 (2-0)
Sat, Oct 9	@ Kentucky	W 37-34	6-0 (3-0)
Sat, Oct 16	vs. #12 Arkansas	W 65-43	7-0 (4-0)
Sat, Oct 23	vs. #6 LSU	W 24-17	8-0 (5-0)
Sat, Oct 30	@ Mississippi	W 51-31	9-0 (6-0)
Sat, Nov 6	vs. Chattanooga	W 62-24	10-0 (6-0)
Sat, Nov 13	vs. Georgia	W 49-31	11-0 (7-0)
Fri, Nov 26	@ #11 Alabama	W 28-27	12-0 (8-0)

SEC Championship Game (Atlanta, GA)

Sat, Dec 4	vs. #19 South Carolina	W 56-17	13-0 (9-0)

Tostitos BCS National Championship Game (Glendale, AZ)

Mon, Jan 10	vs. #2 Oregon	W 22-19	14-0 (9-0)

Appendix Two:
2010 Auburn Tigers – Selected Statistics

TEAM AVERAGES

PASSING YARDS	214.4	POINTS FOR	41.2
RUSHING YARDS	284.8	POINTS AGAINST	24.1

PASSING	CMP	ATT	YDS	TD	INT	RAT
C. Newton *	185	280	2854	30	7	182.0
Barrett Trotter	6	9	64	0	0	126.4
Neil Caudle	1	1	42	0	0	452.8
Kodi Burns	2	5	42	1	0	176.6

RUSHING	CAR	YDS	AVG	LONG	TD
Cameron Newton	264	1473	5.6	71	20
Michael Dyer **	182	1093	6.0	38	5
Onterio McCalebb	95	810	8.5	70	9
Mario Fannin	61	395	6.5	42	5
Terrell Zachery	11	71	6.5	31	0

RECEIVING	REC	YDS	AVG	TD
Darvin Adams	52	963	18.5	7
Terrell Zachery	43	605	14.1	4
Emory Blake	33	554	16.8	8
Philip Lutzenkirchen	15	185	12.3	5
Kodi Burns	11	177	16.1	1
Mario Fannin	17	173	10.2	2
Quindarius Carr	3	103	34.3	2
Onterio McCalebb	7	86	12.3	1
Eric Smith	5	49	9.8	0
Derek Winter	3	44	14.7	0
Cameron Newton	2	42	21.0	1

KICKING	XPM	XPA	FGM	FGA	PTS
Wes Byrum	72	73	17	22	123

* 1st *Nationally in Passing Efficiency*
** *Set Auburn freshman rushing record*

Appendix Three:
2010 Auburn Tigers – AP Ranking by Week

Preseason:	22	
Week 2 (Sept. 5):	21	
Week 3 (Sept. 12):	16	
Week 4 (Sept. 19):	17	
Week 5 (Sept. 26):	10	
Week 6 (Oct. 3):	8	
Week 7 (Oct. 10):	7	
Week 8 (Oct. 17):	5	(BCS: 4)
Week 9 (Oct. 24):	3	(BCS: 1)
Week 10 (Oct. 31):	3	(BCS: 2)
Week 11 (Nov. 7):	2	(BCS: 2)
Week 12 (Nov. 14):	2	(BCS: 2)
Week 13 (Nov. 21):	2	(BCS: 2)
Week 14 (Nov. 29):	2	(BCS: 1)
Week 15 (Dec. 5):	1	(BCS: 1)
Final Rankings (Postseason)	1	(BCS: 1)

Appendix Four:
Years Auburn Can Claim a National Championship*

1910   6-1; outscored opponents 176-9

1913   (*College Football Research Center*, among others)
8-0; outscored opponents 224-13

1914   (*James Howell Computer Rankings*)
8-0-1; outscored opponents 193-0**

1957   (*Associated Press*)
10-0; outscored opponents 207-28
did not play in postseason due to probation

1958   9-0-1; outscored opponents 173-62

1983   (*New York Times*)
11-1; defeated Michigan in Sugar Bowl, 9-7

1993   (*Harry Frye; Jason S. Martin; National Championship
Foundation; Nutshell Sports; Sparks Achievement; David
Wilson*)
11-0; *did not play in postseason due to probation*

2004   (*Trexler; Kiser; RPI; MCubed; EFI; GBEldredge; Fanspoll PNC*)
13-0; defeated Virginia Tech in Sugar Bowl, 16-13

2010   (*BCS; AP; USA Today*; etc.)
14-0; defeated #2 Oregon in BCS National Championship
Game, 22-19

**Using the method pioneered by certain other universities of
claiming any title that can remotely be claimed, as awarded by any
organization, no matter how well-recognized (or not), even
retroactively.*
**The draw was by a score of 0-0.

ABOUT THE AUTHORS

Van Allen Plexico managed to attend Auburn (and score student football tickets) for some portion of every year between 1986 and 1996. He realizes that's probably not something one should brag about, but hey. He teaches college near St Louis (because ten years as a student was somehow just not enough time to spend at school) and writes and edits for a variety of publishers. Find links to his various projects at *www.plexico.net*.

John Ringer graduated from Auburn in 1991 (which may be the greatest time ever to be an Auburn student – SEC titles in 1987, 88 and 89 and the 1989 Iron Bowl). His family has had season tickets every year since well before he was born and he grew up wandering around Jordan-Hare on game days. He currently lives in Richmond, Virginia where he spends way too much time reading about college football on the internet and teaching his children to love Auburn football.

Made in the USA
Lexington, KY
18 March 2011